James T Goudie

Notes and Gleanings

Being leaves from the diary of a voyage to and from Australia and New Zealand, in

1893

James T Goudie

Notes and Gleanings
Being leaves from the diary of a voyage to and from Australia and New Zealand, in 1893

ISBN/EAN: 9783337016005

Printed in Europe, USA, Canada, Australia, Japan

Cover: Foto ©Andreas Hilbeck / pixelio.de

More available books at **www.hansebooks.com**

NOTES AND GLEANINGS

NOTES AND GLEANINGS

BEING

LEAVES FROM THE DIARY OF A VOYAGE
TO AND FROM AUSTRALIA AND
NEW ZEALAND, IN 1893

BY

JAMES T. GOUDIE, J.P., F.S.A. Scot.

"Nothing extenuate, nor set down aught in malice."—*Othello*

PRINTED BY R. & R. CLARK, EDINBURGH,
FOR PRIVATE CIRCULATION ONLY
1894

PREFACE

IN preparing for printing these extracts from my Diary, I have selected only what I think may be of interest to my personal friends, for whom this little volume is intended. The names of many of our friends with whom we spent pleasant days and evenings have been omitted, because, although we shall always remember them with the kindliest feelings, their names could not be of interest to most of our friends at home.

I have noted only the subjects and objects which interested us from day to day, and some leading particulars regarding the Colonies in which we spent a delightful holiday. For statistical information and details as to government, trade, and social economics in the different Colonies, I have drawn largely upon *The Victorian Year Book*, compiled by H. H. Hayter, Esq., Government Statist of Victoria; *Estimates of Revenue and Expenditure of the Colony of Victoria*, 1893; *The Wealth and Progress of New South Wales*, 1892, compiled by T. A. Coghlan, Esq., Government Statist of New South Wales;

Estimates of the Ways and Means of the Government of New South Wales for the Year 1893; *The Tasmanian Official Record*, compiled by the Government Statist, Mr. Johnston; *The Government Statistics of New Zealand*, 1892, and other publications kindly supplied to me by the Agents-general for the various Colonies, and by some colonial friends.

Though under temporary depression at the time of my visit, there is no doubt that a great future is before these Colonies. Whether as independent states, or as continuing to form part of Greater Britain, they cannot fail to occupy an important position; and their fortunes cannot be matter of indifference to citizens of the old country, especially to those connected with colonial trade. If any of my friends who may peruse the following pages should be induced to visit those distant regions, whether for business or pleasure, or, as in my own case, for both combined, they may be assured of a cordial reception, and of a lifelong gratification as the result.

J. T. G.

OAKLEIGH PARK,
POLLOKSHIELDS, GLASGOW,
May 1894.

CONTENTS

CHAPTER I
LONDON TO EGYPT . . . . PAGE 1

CHAPTER II
PORT SAID TO MELBOURNE . . 22

CHAPTER III
MELBOURNE 40

CHAPTER IV
TASMANIA 48

CHAPTER V
NEW ZEALAND 52

CHAPTER VI
SYDNEY 104

CHAPTER VII
QUEENSLAND 108

	PAGE
CHAPTER VIII	
New South Wales	115
CHAPTER IX	
Victoria	132
CHAPTER X	
South Australia	141
CHAPTER XI	
Australian Banking and Finance . .	145
CHAPTER XII	
Homeward	160

NOTES AND GLEANINGS

CHAPTER I

LONDON TO EGYPT

A LONG business connection with the Australasian Colonies had often made me wish to visit those interesting parts of the world; but the constant attention required by a wide-spread business at home and abroad is not easily set aside; and I had to defer my visit until I felt sure that every one of my principal assistants could manage the departments under their charge to my satisfaction and advantage, and until my eldest son should be of age, and able to act for me in private matters of business.

Having made all necessary arrangements, I left home on the 30th January 1893 by Midland Railway for London, where I had some business matters to arrange, and friends to see before leaving. My wife and two of my daughters, who were to accompany me, followed on the 2nd February.

At Liverpool Street Station, from which we left for the Royal Albert Docks, we were met by several of our esteemed colonial friends resident in London, among these being Mr. Ewen, Mr. and Mrs. Nichol, and Mr. Webster, and from them received the first indication of the intensely friendly reception we afterwards met with everywhere throughout the Colonies.

We sailed in the *Oceana*, one of the largest and newest of the P. & O. Company's fleet of magnificent steamers, of 6362 tons, and 7500 horse-power, and with a crew of 298 all told.

Over three hundred passengers embarked at the docks, and the scene was one of the most interesting I ever witnessed.

Some were starting on a voyage for the benefit of their health, and were parting from their loved ones with many misgivings. Sons were leaving their parents for distant and, in some cases, unhealthy climates. Brothers and sisters who had been spending a short time at home, after long absence, were again parting, perhaps for ever. Military officers who had been home on sick leave from India were again leaving their families and friends to face the same trying circumstances which had nearly proved fatal to them before. Several young professional men were sailing for

Australia and New Zealand to found homes and reputations for themselves, and college friends were wishing them a hearty " God-speed." Young ladies and gentlemen who had been in England at schools and colleges were in buoyant spirits at the prospect of returning to their homes and friends. And many, like ourselves, who were embarking on a voyage for pleasure, were in high spirits, anticipating pleasures from scenes and scenery new and interesting to us, although not without some feelings of apprehension regarding the perils of the sea and the approach of *mal-de-mer*.

At 12 o'clock prompt the ship's bell was rung, and "All-ashore" sounded along the decks. Final leave-takings ended, the gangways were withdrawn, mooring ropes thrown off, the powerful engines set the screw in motion, and the great ship moved off on another of her prosperous voyages. We soon found order and discipline reigned on board. The luggage which had been brought with the passengers, and had been put in heaps on the deck, was soon all arranged in the berths by the active stewards, with the accuracy of letter-sorters.

Two unusual incidents happened to us at the beginning of the voyage. First, the machinery for moving the dock gates had got out of order, and we did not get out of the docks till two hours after our time; and then, owing to the delay, we grounded on a mudbank in the river, and did not get off till 10.30 P.M. The night was fine, and with a light breeze of south-east wind, we sailed along the Essex coast as smoothly as if we had been in a canal.

Saturday the 4th February, our first day at sea, was one of those charming early spring days so common in the south of England.

The wind was very light, the sea smooth, and our good ship travelled along at nearly sixteen knots per hour. The sky was almost cloudless overhead, sea-birds hovered around us, the Channel was dotted over with the white sails of vessels, large and small. The shores of our dear island home were on our right, the coast of France on our left, and the pleasures of motion, which a good sailor like myself feels, formed a charming prelude to a voyage which I shall ever remember with the greatest pleasure.

At 4.30 in the afternoon places at the tables for the remainder of the voyage were arranged, the knowing ones securing that part of the saloon where the motion of the ship is least felt. In no case did we hear of any who were placed at the same table becoming disagreeable to each other, but in many cases friendships were formed there which will be lasting and pleasant.

At 7 or 7.30 A.M., as desired, tea or coffee is handed into passengers' berths; at 8.30 the awakening bugle is sounded, and at 9.30 breakfast is served; luncheon is at 1 P.M., tea at 4, and dinner at 6.30 P.M. Hot or cold baths can be had at any hour from 6 A.M. to 6 P.M.

Before 7 P.M. we had passed the Isle of Wight, and were heading for Ushant, on the French coast, and some of us were beginning to feel the effects of the open sea. Some of the lady passengers did not feel inclined to take their places at the dinner table, but my wife and girls enjoyed their second dinner as much as they had enjoyed their first, when we were lying at anchor in the Thames.

Every part of the steamer was brilliantly lighted with electric light. It was interesting to watch how the passengers began to gather into small groups, in the music saloon, on the deck, in the smoking-room, and elsewhere, and how the natural reserve of people thrown together on board ship gave way to the desire to be agreeable. Preliminary talks on the prospects of the voyage, and other matters common to all, served to introduce people to each other, and enabled them to form opinions as to how far they would be agreeable companions. Life on board a large passenger steamer is very much like life in a large Continental hotel, where most of the people one meets have travelled a good deal, and know much of men and countries. Lights are extinguished in the saloons and berths at 11 P.M., but all the passages are well lighted during the whole night.

The morning of Sunday the 5th February was fine, with the wind from the south-east; and by noon our run for the twenty-four hours was 367 miles. The rule regarding divine service on board the P. & O. Company's steamers is, that the Church of England service is read in the first saloon at 10.45 A.M., and a Presbyterian service is held in the second saloon at 8 P.M., both classes of passengers joining in the services. We had six parsons on board, all missionaries I understood, and bent on doing good to the heathen; but I was surprised to hear how general was the opinion of people long resident in India and China, that more good might be done at home by the men and money devoted to missionary enterprises abroad, and that missionary work, in China particularly, had, up till now, been only a small success.

The wind in the afternoon changed to south-west, and by 8 P.M. we had quite a gale; and most of the ladies and many of the gentlemen had come to the conclusion that their own cabins were the most comfortable part of the ship on a Sunday evening, and they had therefore retired to their seclusion. But if one happened to be passing, painfully audible sounds indicated that they were not quite happy even there.

By Monday morning the wind had gone down, and although there was a heavy swell in the Bay of Biscay, most of the passengers were able to be on deck.

A meeting of gentlemen was held in the forenoon to form an entertainments committee, and a list of subscriptions was taken up for prizes to be afterwards competed for.

The games consisted of chess, draughts, whist, backgammon, quoits, egg and spoon, and potato and bucket races, tug-of-war, chalking the pig's eye, cock-fighting, etc. etc., several of which were very amusing. My girls won several prizes, and I won the draughts match.

Nearly all the ladies were able to be at dinner; and in the evening the first concert was given in the second saloon, to which the first saloon passengers were invited. The entertainment was very enjoyable, particularly the recitations given by Captain Speedie, who was appointed, by the British Government, guardian to the son of King Theodore of Abyssinia after the Abyssinian war.

Early on Tuesday morning we had crossed the Bay and passed Cape St. Vincent. By 10.30 A.M. we were off Trafalgar Bay, of glorious memory, and about the same time we caught a glimpse (our first) of Africa, having sighted Cape Martel on the coast of Tangiers. About 1 P.M. we passed the old fortified town of Teneriffa, once a

Moorish stronghold, on the coast of Spain, and even now a place of importance as a fortified town. At 3 P.M. we had done 1299 miles of our journey, and anchored in the Bay of Gibraltar.

The Rock, as it is usually called, is a hill of limestone, rising to an altitude of 1437 feet at the highest point. Its length is about three miles, and its breadth three-quarters of a mile. The side facing the Mediterranean and the end towards the sandy isthmus which connects it with Spain, are both very precipitous, and along the end toward the Straits, and the side facing the Bay, there is a fringe of somewhat level ground, on which the town is built. The whole frontage along the shore is lined with batteries, in tiers, one above the other, mounting guns of all sizes from one hundred tons downwards; and in the face of the hill above the town are many openings through which immense guns project. The perpendicular rock towards Spain has tier over tier of gun ports, and even on the Mediterranean side, which is quite inaccessible, guns are largely in evidence. The plan of the great chambers hewn out of the rock and other particulars of the fortifications are said to be known only to the authorities on the Rock. The number of guns in the fortifications is over a thousand. The civil population at present is about 9000, and the military population averages about 4000. The population is a very mixed one, composed of British, Spanish, Moorish, and Portuguese residents. Each foreign element has its own quarters and bazaar or shops. There is only one street in the town, narrow lanes crossing at right angles. The harbour is a fine bay, six by four miles. We went ashore and drove through the town to the frontier of Spain. There is a neutral zone of half a mile between the sentry posts, which is used as a recreation ground. We also drove to Europa Point, where the lighthouse and infantry barracks are, and from which we had a fine view across the Straits, which are about eleven miles wide to the African shore, and across the Bay to the shores of Spain. Gibraltar and the rocky promontory on the African coast opposite, called Cape Ceuta, were in ancient times called the Pillars of Hercules.

Gibraltar has been a fortress from remote antiquity. It was a stronghold of the Tyrians or Carthaginians, and was seized by the Moors on their first incursion into Spain. It was strongly fortified by Charles V. It was taken possession of by the British in 1704, in whose possession it has remained ever since. It is now one of the most important fortifications which guard our way to India by the Suez Canal, and an evidence of the power which Britain has acquired and wields on the globe. It was dark when we left Gibraltar, about 7 P.M. Tuesday had been a charming day with a bright sun and a temperature of 61°.

On the morning of the 8th we were within sight of the coast of Algiers. The sky was cloudless, and the temperature 63° at 9 A.M.; the lovely blue of the Mediterranean Sea was most striking when the rays of the morning sun touched it in an oblique direction. Ladies were now walking the deck in summer dresses, and gentlemen in flannel suits and straw hats. Many sailing vessels were within sight, and the dark outlines of the African mountains between us and the cloudless horizon looked soft and peaceful. The afternoon was equally fine, and the first series of games was played. In the evening we had a most enjoyable concert.

Thursday the 9th was cold and cloudy, and at 9 A.M. the temperature was only 57°, we being within the influence of the snow-capped mountains of Algeria, which we could see at a great distance. We did not expect to see snow-covered mountains in Africa, that continent being generally associated in our minds with excessive heat.

Inexperienced travellers were, at 10.30 A.M., much alarmed by the furious ringing of the bells, and the rushing of the crew to the boats, untying their ropes, and preparing to lower them; but we were reassured when we were told it was only drill. There are printed rules regarding emergencies hung up in the main saloon stair, and every officer has his appointed place, and every one of the crew knows which boat to lower and man—thus avoiding confusion in case of an accident. But I would not put much trust in the Lascar sailors in a case of real danger. They were nearly all small men, of low physique, and few of them could speak English. They were under petty officers of their own class, called Sarangs, and did the cleaning of brass, and painted wood well, but as seamen—no.

There were 171 of these men in a crew of 298. They are paid twenty rupees per month. After a fine run of 372 miles for the day we passed the lights of Tunis about 9 P.M.

When I came on deck at 8.45 A.M. on the 10th, we were abreast of the small island of Gozo, called Gaulos by the Romans. It is a very interesting place, having many Roman monuments, including the walls of the Giant's Tower; and there is a British fort on it called the Fort of Rabetto.

Malta is 984 miles from Gibraltar, and we did the distance in two days eighteen hours. The principal town in Malta is Valetta, the harbour of which is our chief naval station in the Mediterranean, and it is so fortified that it is considered impregnable.

Inside the principal entrance the harbour is

divided into two bays, called the Grand Harbour and the Quarantine Harbour, and the entrances of these again are strongly fortified. Between these bays, on a tongue of the land, is built the town of Valetta, which is about two miles long and two-thirds of a mile broad, and the ground rises so abruptly from the water that many of the streets are practically flights of stairs. The landward end of the town is protected by several lines of walls and batteries.

Malta is enormously interesting, historically. It is thought by some to have been the "Hyperion" of Homer, but there is little doubt it was colonised by the Phœnicians 1500 years before the Christian era. The Greeks took possession of it about 700 years B.C., and they in turn were driven out by the Carthaginians about 200 years later. The Romans were in possession of it 200 years afterwards, and they valued it highly as a commercial centre, and for its fine linen and cotton fabrics, manufactured then, as now, by the Maltese. In the fifth century it was held by the Vandals and the Goths respectively. For three centuries later it formed part of the Byzantine Empire. In 870 A.D. the Arabs took possession of it, and it remained under their control for 200 years, when Count Roger of Sicily drove the Arabs out, and established a popular council for the government of the island. It was under the sovereignty of several states, but had the same form of local government till 1530, when it was taken possession of by the Emperor Charles V., and by him granted in perpetual sovereignty to the Knights of St. John of Jerusalem, whom the Turks had recently driven from Rhodes. The Knights at once began to fortify Valetta, and by 1565 their fortifications were strong enough to repel the Turks, who then, and in 1571, attempted to take possession of the island.

The Knights were masters of the island till 1798, when the first Napoleon got possession of it by treachery. But a few months later the Maltese rose against the French, and with the assistance of the British drove them out; and by the Treaty of Vienna in 1801 it was recognised as a British possession. We found the public buildings very interesting, most of them having been built by the Knights. The building formerly the Palace of the Grand Master is now the residence of the Governor of the island. It is an unpretentious building outside, but internally is a superb edifice. The armoury is a hall 253 feet long by 38 broad, and it contains a wonderful collection of arms and weapons, some of a date previous to the removal of the Knights from Rhodes to Malta. The Council Hall is hung with magnificent tapestries representing the four great continents of the world, and the roof is adorned with fine frescoes.

The country palace of the Grand Master is now the country residence of the Governor. It has beautiful gardens, and the orange and lemon trees were loaded with fruit when we visited them.

The Church of Saint John, built by the Knights in 1578, is a magnificent building inside. It has a beautiful arched roof, decorated with panels in relief, and the floor is covered with coats of arms of the Knights. The chapels round the church are in the usual style, and have rich lamps and furniture. Another interesting church is that of Saint Paul, built in the shape of a Maltese cross. Internally it is very plain, the only object of interest in it being a statue of the saint in a Roman dress and glazed felt hat, such as was worn by sailors in the navy *twenty-five* years ago. The barracks, hospitals, and other military buildings, are nearly all structures of last century. The island, mostly composed of limestone rocks, is flat, the highest point being only 590 feet, and the landscape very uninteresting. Originally, there was so little soil on the island that large quantities were brought from Sicily; but where there is sufficient soil it is very productive, the vegetable products being much the same as in Italy, with the addition of the sugar-cane.

We dined ashore while our vessel was taking in coals, and in the evening went to the Government Theatre. By the special request of our captain, an opera was performed, for the enjoyment of the *Oceana's* passengers. The singing was good; the acting indifferent.

We left Valetta at midnight, and met a good strong breeze outside the harbour, but the sea was comparatively smooth. The next stage of our journey was to Brindisi, a distance of 360 miles, and the morning of the 11th found us sailing along the coast of Sicily, the largest island in the Mediterranean. Its population is over two and a half millions. The landscape near the coast presents a beautiful combination of hill and valley, while in the distance towers Mount Etna, 10,840 feet above the sea. Near the top it was covered with snow, and the only indication we could see of its character was a column of steam rising from the crater. According to Sir Charles Lyell, the geology of the island is most remarkable. It has emerged from the Mediterranean since that sea was peopled with all the existing species of shells and zoophytes, and the beds of the marine strata are a marked feature in the formation of the island.

The soil of Sicily is very fertile. Livy spoke of it as the granary of the Romans. Its vineyards cover nearly 500,000, and its olive gardens nearly 150,000, acres. It also produces flax, hemp, and cotton; and its shores are the happy hunting-ground of the coral fishers. In prehistoric times it was inhabited by a people who were called Siculi, but the actual history of the island only begins with the establishment of Greek and Phœnician colonies in the eighth century B.C., from which time until it became a Roman province in the year 210 B.C. the names of many heroes of ancient renown, among them Hippocrates, Dionysius, and Pyrrhus, were associated with it; and Verres, said to be "damned to everlasting fame," in the orations of Cicero, was Governor of it in 70-73 B.C. In the fifth century it was taken possession of by the Vandals, passing afterwards into the hands of the Ostrogoths, who retained it till the year 535 A.D., when it was annexed to the Byzantine Empire. It was invaded by the Saracens in 827 A.D., and after passing through various political vicissitudes, it was under Norman rule from 1072 to 1194, from which to 1258 its political history is the same as that of Naples. It was more or less under the government of the representatives of the royal families of Spain and Austria, with the exception of a short period, from 1806 to 1815, when Joseph Bonaparte and Joachim Murat ruled it as kings, down to 1860, when it was annexed to the Kingdom of Italy under Victor Emmanuel. The mountains in the interior were covered with snow, and the temperature on board our steamer was

only 51° at mid-day. We arrived at Brindisi at
8.30 A.M. on Sunday the 12th. Although the
harbour has been deepened and a fine quay constructed for the accommodation of the large mail-
steamers, the town itself is only of third rate
importance as even Italian towns of the present
day go, and is as dirty as such towns usually are.
It has a decayed appearance, and there seemed
to be very little local traffic. Originally a
Tarentine colony, called Brundisium, it was taken
possession of by the Romans 245 B.C. It was
at one time the chief station of the Roman fleet,
and the termination of the great Appian Way,
or southern road from Rome. It was also the
chief point of departure for Greece and the East.
From it the Crusaders embarked; and it was here
that Virgil died in the year 19 B.C. In the days
of Horace it took as long to travel from Rome to
Brindisi as it does from London to Brindisi now.
There are few objects of interest in the town.
The cathedral in which Frederick II. married
Yolanda, in 1225, is still in existence, but in a
dilapidated condition. There is a marble column
fifty feet high, near the harbour, by some said to
mark the termination of the Appian Way, and by
others to have been part of a pagan temple. A
castle, commenced by Frederick II. and finished
by Charles V., is still partially occupied; and
there are the remains of the wall of the old

town, which was destroyed by an earthquake in 1456.

We spent all Sunday at Brindisi waiting the mails; and the weather was lovely. A very good band played on the quay until they had exhausted the contributions of the passengers, and then they played *Ta-ra-ra-boom-de-ay* and retired. Having got 730 sacks of mails on board, we left Brindisi at 3.30 A.M. on Monday the 13th for Port Said, a distance of 930 miles. Next afternoon we passed the Ionian Islands, but so far off that we could not see them to the advantage which we did on our way home, and I will therefore leave the description of them to that part of our voyage.

Tuesday morning was fine, and about 9 A.M. we were in full view of the mountains of Crete, which rise to a height of 7674 feet. They were covered with snow, and look beautiful in the early morning light. The population of Crete now is said to be only one-tenth of what it was under the Romans. Its prosperity steadily declined under the Venetians, the Egyptians, and the Turks. Along its shores Paul sailed on his way to Rome. The weather continued lovely, and under its influence every one seemed to be enjoying the voyage, and a general feeling of harmony appeared to have established itself among the passengers, all doing their best to be agreeable to their neighbours. The popular officers of the ship also contributed much to the enjoyment of the voyage, leading or joining in most of the games.

We had our first dance that evening. The deck in front of the music saloon was covered with an awning, the sides of the space curtained round with white canvas, and the whole profusely decorated with flags, stands of arms, and coloured lamps. The temperature at 7 P.M. was 60° on deck; the ship's band played lively airs, the place was brilliantly lighted with electric light, a refreshment buffet and lounging chairs were conveniently placed for the revival of tired dancers, and even dimly-lighted places were to be found for those inclined to a little flirtation; and that failing of human nature is never absent from such gatherings, even on board ship. The whole arrangements gave satisfaction, and a most enjoyable evening was brought to a close at 11 P.M., making every one feel that life on the ocean wave can be made thoroughly enjoyable in spite of some drawbacks.

The forenoon of the 13th was calm, the sea smooth, and the blue waters of the Mediterranean canopied over by a cloudless sky, and dotted over with the white sails of vessels of all sizes. Two or three whales were sporting round us; the long trail of white foam from our propeller lay like a stream of silver lace on the azure surface of the waveless sea; and the exhilarating feeling caused by our surroundings and the motion of the ship sent a thrill of pleasure through every one never to be forgotten. In the afternoon we sighted Cape Damietta at the mouth of the Nile. The sea being smooth, we could distinguish the water discharged from the river, by its colour, for twenty miles off the shore. At 4.30 we reached Port Said, at the entrance to the Suez Canal. It is a town of 17,000 inhabitants, built on the sand dug out of the canal; its streets are unpaved and dirty, and the houses are built of wood, and look like enormous packing-cases, except a few public buildings with a little pretence to architectural effect, but they are more picturesque than beautiful. The inhabitants are mostly of the lowest type of humanity, and are composed of Egyptians, Negroes, Arabs, and Europeans of the worst class. Here we had our first experience of Eastern life. As soon as we landed we were surrounded by half-clothed Arabs, offering for sale all sorts of rubbishy curios of Japanese and Cingalese manufacture, Moorish embroideries, cigars and cigarettes, etc., and men offering donkeys for a ride into the country or through the town; and the noise made by these men, and the way in which they pushed their wares and their donkeys on our attention, was almost unbearable. There is a mosque of moderate size in the town which we went to see. Large straw shoes are put over people's boots before they are allowed to enter the building, and these being all engaged before my turn came, an official put a piece of matting on one of my feet, and a dirty handkerchief on the other, to keep the floor from being contaminated by Christian touch. The interior of the building possessed no feature of interest. There were a few poor people saying their prayers, and as many priests waiting to receive their offerings, but no form of worship such as we practise is ever held in mosques.

Port Said, named after Said Pasha, the Viceroy who granted the concession for, and took an active interest in making the Suez Canal, is said to be the largest coaling station in the world, over a million tons of coal being supplied to steamers annually. Coals were carried on board our steamer by Arabs in fig-leaf costume, and a man with a whip in his hand kept the carriers up to time in good Egyptian fashion. All the officials are Egyptians. A fresh-water canal from the Nile had to be made to supply the labourers with water while the Suez Canal works were in progress, and Port Said is well supplied with water from it. Having completed our coaling, and fixed our electric apparatus to light us through the canal, we left for Suez at 7 P.M.

CHAPTER II

PORT SAID TO MELBOURNE

THE Suez Canal is cut through a desert of sand, and not a scrap of vegetation is to be seen along its whole course, except at points where the fresh-water canal which supplies the stations with water comes near it. It is 112 yards wide at the surface of the water, 26 yards wide at the bottom, and 30 feet deep. The height of the banks varies from 30 to 85 feet, and where the banks are highest the width of the cutting at the top is 173 yards. About half through the canal is a series of lakes, called Timsah, Menzaleh, and Abu Ballah, or the Bitter Lakes, and these are believed to have formed part of the Red Sea when the Israelites went out of Egypt, and their passage across is supposed to have been near what is now called Lake Timsah, which is twenty miles from the Red Sea. The great road from Egypt to the east crosses the canal, a short distance from Timsah, and we saw a large caravan of pilgrims on their way to Mecca resting on a sandy plain near the ferry. The water of the Red Sea is six and a half feet higher than that of the Mediterranean, but owing to the length of the canal there is practically no current in it, the movement of the water not being noticeable beyond the lakes. The length of the canal is 87 French miles. We took twenty-two hours to pass through it. Except when passing through the lakes, the speed of steamers must not exceed five miles per hour. The canal enters the Red Sea several miles below the town of Suez, and we only remained an hour at Port Suez to take some mails and a few passengers on board. Shortly after starting again we passed "Moses' Well," marked by a clump of palm-trees on a sandy plain, near the sea-shore. From London to Suez is 3657 miles.

Friday the 17th, our first day in the Red Sea, was delightful. A fine breeze of north-east wind kept the temperature down to 78°. In the evening we had our first fancy dress ball. Many of our passengers had brought fancy dresses with them, and others had bought outfits at Port Said, while officers and others holding official appointments dressed in uniform, giving the company a picturesque appearance. The ball-*room* was arranged as before, and the dance was as successful as our first one.

On Saturday the 18th we had a light breeze of south-east wind, the temperature at 9 A.M. 82°.

The water of the Red Sea at this part is of the same deep blue as that of the Mediterranean. Off Jedda we passed a sailing ship conveying pilgrims to Mecca. There was a good deal of interest taken in our daily runs, and what are called "Calcutta sweepstakes" were indulged in daily, the arrangements being that one of the officers gave the approximate length of our run for the day, and then an auctioneer was appointed to sell numbers from 10 above to 10 below the expected run, the purchaser of the winning number getting all the money given for the other numbers, which sometimes amounted to over twenty pounds.

On Sunday the 19th we had a strong breeze of wind and a choppy sea. In the forenoon we passed a group of islands called the Twelve Apostles, and in the afternoon an island called Zuco, famous for antelopes, and as a rendezvous for dealers in slaves some years ago.

We arrived at Aden, 1308 miles from Suez, at 7.30 A.M. on the 20th. It has a striking resemblance to Gibraltar, and is one of the strongest and most important military and naval stations on our way to India. Like Gibraltar, Aden is a rocky peninsula, projecting about five miles from the coast of Arabia, and connected to it by a low isthmus about three-quarters of a mile wide. It is of volcanic origin, and the town stands on an old crater: the rocks round it are bleak, bare, and barren, and rise to a height of 1776 feet above the sea. Previous to the discovery of the passage to India by the Cape, it was a place of military importance and great trade, and in the seventeenth century it had a population of twenty-five thousand, but in 1839, when it was taken possession of by the East India Company, the population had dwindled down to seven hundred. It has now risen to thirty thousand. The great tanks, supposed to have been constructed in the sixth or seventh century, are the only objects of interest worth seeing in the peninsula.

As soon as our anchor was down, large numbers of Arab men and boys crowded on board, selling antelopes' horns, tiger skins, ostrich feathers, etc., asking 20s. and taking 5s. for an article. Their only covering was a piece of cloth round the loins. Men and boys, in canoes hollowed out of trunks of trees, swarmed round our ship, and dived for coins thrown overboard by the passengers, which they invariably caught before they sank out of reach. The scene was altogether indescribable. Aden is very hot, but not unhealthy. We took on board a number of passengers from Bombay, who were considered stiff and formal. The temperature when we left at 2.30 P.M. was 87°. From Aden to Colombo is 2093 miles.

Tuesday the 21st, we were sailing down the

Gulf of Aden; and passed Cape Guardafui at 4 P.M., the weather being fine, and the temperature at 6 P.M. 82°.

There was another dance in the evening. About 11 P.M. we saw the Southern Cross for the first time. It is a very ordinary constellation, nothing like the pictures of it in astronomical books, and requires a good deal of imagination to form it into a cross. More interesting was the appearance of the new moon, which lay horizontal like the letter ⌣. On Wednesday the 22nd we had a fine breeze and a temperature of 82°. The *Australia*, one of the P. and O. Company's steamers, passed us on her homeward voyage. We had another concert in the evening, but it was a formal affair.

The 23rd was another charming day, and games for prizes were played; my daughter Grace won the buckets game, and I won the draughts match. Before leaving home I expected to read a great deal during the voyage, but time was passing so pleasantly that reading seemed a toil, and during the three weeks I had been at sea I had not read one book through.

Friday the 24th was another charming day, the temperature 83° at noon. In the evening the stewards gave a negro entertainment, which was very good, and much enjoyed.

Sunday the 26th, at 7.30 A.M., we arrived at

Colombo, the chief town in Ceylon. We landed at 9 A.M., and here, *to us*, a new world opened, although an old world as it existed thousands of years ago. The race of people we had not seen before, and their modes of life were new to us. Their dresses, houses, and all their surroundings were of a kind we had not even thought of; and no one can convey by pen a correct idea of the peculiar beauty of the landscape.

The greater part of the Cingalese are descendants of colonists from the valley of the Ganges, who settled in the island 500 years B.C. They are very effeminate in appearance, both men and women having delicate features and slender forms.

The dress of the poorer class of men consists of a waist-cloth, called a camboy, only, and their hair is combed back from their foreheads and twisted in a knot at the back of their heads, and fastened with combs. The women of the same class wear a short skirt, and a loose jacket of white or printed cotton, and adorn themselves with jewellery. Their hair is worn in the same way as the men's. They carry water in brown clay pots on their heads, as in the days of the Pharaohs; and the men carry their burdens suspended from yokes on their shoulders. Their houses are built of mud, and roofed with palm leaves, and their food consists of rice and fruit chiefly. The better class, males and females, dress in skirts and jackets of white linen, and wear white caps, making it very difficult for strangers to detect the males from the females. The children up to about seven years of age do not wear any clothing.

Buddhism is the religion of the large majority of the natives. No worship is offered to Budda as a deity. He is regarded as a type of earthly goodness and wisdom only, deserving of imitation. We engaged a carriage for the day, the charge being six rupees, and having driven for an hour through the town to see the most interesting parts of it, we drove seven miles into the country to a place called Mount Lavinia, where there is a very nice hotel on the sea-shore. We had a splendidly-cooked and well-served luncheon there for two rupees each. The road was through an avenue of palms, the palmyra and areca being next in number to the cocoa-nut palm, and the bread-fruit and banana trees were also abundant. Many trees and flowering shrubs, of which we did not know the names, filled the spaces between the palms, while crotons and similar plants, which require careful treatment in hothouses at home, grew by the roadside like brackens. Most of the vegetation was new to us, and the marvellous beauty of the avenue through which we drove into the country I cannot possibly describe. The cocoa-nut palm rises to a height of over 100 feet, and there are no leaves on it except near the top, and few of them have more than eighteen or twenty leaves altogether; each leaf is about fifteen feet long, and curves downward, and every tree produces about one hundred nuts annually. Another tree, which we saw here for the first time, and afterwards in Australia, interested us very much. It is called the papaw tree, is a native of South America, and has the singular property of turning newly-killed poultry or beef tender in a few hours when hung among its leaves.

From the verandah of the hotel we saw the fishermen, in their peculiar boats called catamarans, hauling their nets; and on the rocks, up to their waists in the surf, were numerous native men and boys fishing with rods and lines, the bait being a piece of bright metal, very like the spoon-bait sometimes used to catch sea-trout at home.

On our way back to Colombo we drove through one of the cinnamon gardens, which perfume "the spicy breezes" that "blow soft o'er Ceylon's isle," and found it not over well cultivated. The areca or betel-nut is largely cultivated and used in Ceylon. It is a species of pepper plant, the leaves of which are prepared in a peculiar way, and chewed as tobacco is chewed by some people; it is a strong narcotic, causing giddiness in persons not accustomed to it. It makes the teeth and lips red, and people using it appear to be spitting blood. We were quite satisfied to see it grow without testing its qualities. Pine-apples were growing in the same gardens, and could be bought for twopence each. Beside these gardens is a museum, containing an interesting collection of native birds, which are very beautiful, and animals and minerals, chiefly the productions of the island. All the way from Mount Lavinia the roads were lined with native houses and shops, most of them being sheds formed of upright sticks hung round with cocoa-nut mats, and roofed with strips of bark or leaves. The sides next to the road were open, but nothing whatever in the shape of furniture, except a board for sitting on, could be seen in any of them. The natives nearly all sleep outside.

We entered the town by that part of it called the fort, in which are the Government and military offices, and the residences of most of the British inhabitants, civil and military. The houses are mostly built of stone, and are of European style of architecture, having broad verandahs and overhanging roofs to prevent the rain gaining admission by the windows, which are not filled with glass, but only screened with Venetian blinds. The best shops, European and native, are in this quarter. Colombo is the place to which our soldiers are sent from India to recruit their health, and the barrack accommodation is large. There are also numerous batteries along the shore where artillerymen are quartered. There is a fine supply of water in the town, brought from a range of hills, about thirty miles distant, by the Government. The day had been hot, the temperature in the shade 85°, and even amid all the beauties of tropical vegetation and absolutely new surroundings we felt tired, and were pleased to get on board our ship in time for dinner at 6.30. At 10 P.M. we left for Australia.

Next day, the 27th, was fine, the temperature 82°. Shoals of flying-fish rose from the water like flocks of birds, and after flying a few hundred yards, plunged again into the calm blue sea. Neither vessel nor cloud was to be seen; the ocean around us seemed a perfect circle, and the sky a perfect dome, and our great ship seemed little more than a fly on a circular mirror under a glass shade. But evening brought us back to the realities of life. The amusements committee had arranged to have *tableaux vivants*, the scenes to be from the life of Mary Queen of Scots; but when the distinguished naval officer, who had the arranging of the characters, asked some of the ladies to act the part of waiting-maids, none could be found to represent a part so mean, all wanted to be queens, and the attempt to get up the entertainment ended in a tableau not requiring a rehearsal. After dark we had a magnificent display of tropical lightning. We crossed the line at 6.30 A.M. on the 28th. One or two ladies who came on deck shortly after were anxious to see " the line," and they were gratified by looking through a telescope, across the object glass of which a waggish officer had tied a hair, but they were a good deal annoyed when they found they had only seen a *hair line!* Amusements of all sorts were actively engaged in during the day, although the temperature was 84° in the shade.

The 1st of March was finer than the 1st of July usually is at home. At noon we were in 7° 40′ south latitude, and the sun was nearly overhead, the temperature 85° in the shade, and 115° in the sun. In the afternoon we had some showers, the first rain we had had since we left home. We had a full moon at night, decidedly larger and brighter than ever seen at home. At 6 A.M. on the 2nd we crossed the sun's meridian, and in the afternoon we met the south-east trade winds, which lowered the temperature about 5°, but the weather continued fine.

Our daily run was about 370 miles.

On the evening of the 3rd we had another fancy dress ball, and those best able to judge pronounced the dresses a perfect success, and agreed that all the ladies displayed excellent taste in dressing to suit their figures and style; and many of the gentlemen were highly complimented on their "get-up." Several of the ladies had their hair powdered, and wore black patches, and much might be said in favour of the ladies of past generations who adopted this mode of increasing their charms. Perhaps the sense of novelty was strong, but it seemed to add a charm to many pretty faces. The dresses were so varied, that I do not think the most expert writer for a ladies' journal could have described them; but the effect was most pleasing, and the whole affair a great success.

The morning of the 4th brought a fresh breeze, a falling barometer, and a lower temperature; at noon it was 74° in the shade, the wind increased, and at dinner time there were several vacant chairs. Later in the evening it fell away again. The second saloon passengers had a very fine show of *tableaux vivants* that evening, to which the first saloon passengers were invited.

Sunday the 5th was inspection day again, when we had another opportunity of seeing our crew mustered. The chief engineer and his men were drawn up in line on the port side, aft, and the sailing crew, petty officers, and stewards, were drawn up on the starboard side, while the officers of the ship, the doctor, and purser stood at the

D

stern wheel between the groups. The black men were dressed in white garments of night-shirt shape, with sashes round their waists, and most of them wore embroidered caps. Some of them wore fancy vests, and others coloured sashes, giving them quite a gay appearance, and all the officers and white men were dressed in their best uniforms. The captain, doctor, and purser then walked down the lines, the men saluting. The ceremony being over, every one hurried off to his duty. The captain and the purser inspect the berths daily, to see that they are kept in proper order; and any passengers having anything to complain of must then state their cause of complaint. All the clergymen having left at Colombo, the captain read the service in a very impressive style, and the purser, who had not much of the parson in his nature, read the lessons. In the evening a highly-esteemed Melbourne merchant (Mr. D. Love), gave a very pathetic and touching address in the second saloon, which was filled with both classes of passengers.

Monday the 6th was much colder, the temperature having fallen to 65°. A strong breeze was blowing, and many ladies were unable to be present at either luncheon or dinner.

The 7th brought a heavy cross sea, which indicated that we were nearing land; and albatrosses began to hover around us. They are the largest of web-footed birds, and are of the gull or petrel family. The plumage on the under side of the body and wings is nearly white, and on the upper side of the wings, back, and neck, a dusky brown colour; the spread of the wings is sometimes twelve feet, and the weight of the bird twenty pounds. We were about 100 miles from land when we first saw them. In the afternoon the wind increased to a gale. At 5.30 we sighted Cape Lewen on the west coast of Australia, and were very pleased to see land again, although our time at sea had passed pleasantly. As darkness came on the weather became very wet and foggy, and as there are ridges of rocks running far out from the shore, our ship was hauled off a point or two from the usual course, for safety. The night was very stormy, the lightning most brilliant, and the thunder terrific; but we were all pleased to see a thunder-storm in that latitude.

The morning of the 8th was hazy after the storm, but we came in sight of land again at 8 o'clock, and at 1 o'clock entered King George's Sound, having accomplished 10,488 miles of our journey. What is called the Sound is a fine bay, and the town of Albany, the second city in the colony of Western Australia, is built on the rising ground surrounding it. The population of Albany is under 7000, but it has a thriving appearance, and was interesting to us as the first Australian town we had seen. The houses are nearly all built of wood, but are clean and substantial in appearance. Scottish names predominated on sign-boards over all places of business. There we saw some native Australians. Their skin is darker than that of the Negro race, and they looked like living skeletons. Their limbs are almost straight from above the knees to the ankles, and their arms are the same thickness from the shoulder to the hand; their eyes have less expression than those of monkeys, and their faces are only a little more human like. One of the men we saw was dressed in a suit of moleskin; the other man and the two women and four children were clothed in skins, their legs and arms being bare.

We left Albany for Adelaide, a distance of 1007 miles, at 4.30 P.M. The evening was very pleasant as we steamed round the bold headland, and entered the great Australian Bight.

During the night the wind freshened into a stiff breeze, and in the morning many of our passengers felt more inclined to bed than breakfast when, at 8.30, the bugler wakened the drowsy ones, and annoyed the delicate ones, by playing in the liveliest manner, "Life on the Ocean Wave." By mid-day the breeze had died away, and the temperature had risen to 72°.

Friday the 10th was clear and fine. The

stewards gave a theatrical and musical entertainment in the first saloon in the evening, which was very much enjoyed. Early in the morning of the 11th we passed Kangaroo Island with its abrupt rocky shores, and steered up the Gulf of St. Vincent for Adelaide in one of the finest forenoons we had had since leaving home. The town of Adelaide is eight miles from the sea, and the river on which Port Adelaide is situated is too shallow for the large mail steamers to navigate; consequently all the large steamers anchor in Largo Bay, from which there is a railway to the town.

As we were to be only a few hours in the bay, and intended to visit Adelaide on our way home, we did not go ashore, but we received some letters from friends in Melbourne welcoming us to Australia, and advising us to go to Menzies's Family Hotel when we arrived in Melbourne. Mr., Mrs., and Miss Harvey, the only other passengers from Glasgow, left us here, as they were going to travel north to Sydney by rail, and sail from there to Singapore, Japan, and Vancouver, on their way round the world.

The mails for Melbourne, Sydney, and Brisbane are usually landed at Adelaide, but the workingmen of South Australia will not do any work on Sundays; and as it takes twenty-four hours to go from Adelaide to Melbourne, no trains leave on

Saturday or Sunday for Melbourne, or *vice versa*, and it being Saturday when we arrived, the mails would, if sent ashore, have been kept at Adelaide till Monday at 6.30 P.M. By taking them forward in the steamer they were delivered a day sooner.

We left for Melbourne at 7.30 P.M.

Sunday the 12th was again a beautiful day, and we were sailing along the low sandy coast of South Australia till 1 o'clock, when we passed Discovery Bay, and reached the equally low and uninteresting coast of Victoria. Near Cape Nelson we saw an extensive bush fire, many of which we met with afterwards in New Zealand and elsewhere.

Although the passage had been pleasant, yet most of our passengers, who were nearing their homes, were anxious to get on *terra firma* again, and we also were anxious to get ashore to explore the wonders of the new world. We passed Cape Otway about 6 P.M. on the 12th, and Port Philip Heads at 1 A.M. on Monday the 13th; arriving off Williamstown, the port for Melbourne, at 5 A.M., where we anchored to await the arrival of the port officers. The distance from Adelaide to Melbourne is 485 miles. At 6.30 A.M. the health officers came on board, and it was amusing to see, first the officers and crew, then the second saloon, and then the first saloon passengers, mustered on deck, and counted off like bales of goods. Being all well, we were passed by the doctors, and then taken in hand by the custom house officers, who had to examine our luggage for articles subject to duty. This being almost a matter of form, we were soon allowed to land.

CHAPTER III

MELBOURNE

WILLIAMSTOWN, where the large mail steamers lie, is about five miles from Melbourne, to which we took train, and soon afterwards found ourselves in the city, of which its inhabitants are immensely, and I think rightly, proud. We put up at Menzies's Hotel, as advised by our friends, and found it a well-kept, comfortable house.

We had heard much about colonial hospitality, but we were hardly prepared for the extremely kind reception accorded to us. The colonial papers publish lists of all passengers arriving by the mail steamers, and of strangers arriving in every town by railway, daily, a fact which we did not know, but which accounted for some of our friends calling so soon after our arrival, the first being Sir Frederick and Lady Sargood and two of their daughters.

My first impression of Melbourne was that it was one of the finest cities I had seen; and I have seen most of the large towns in Britain, France, Italy, Belgium, and other countries; but I found, on closer inspection, that the principal streets are not completed as they will be, there being at present six- or seven-story blocks adjoining two- and three-story blocks, which leaves large spaces of rough wall exposed at the ends of the higher buildings, and gives an unfinished appearance to most of the principal thoroughfares. But there are many splendid specimens of architecture among the public and private buildings—some equal to any of their class in Europe. The Bank offices are exceptionally fine buildings, those in Collins Street being much superior to those in Lombard Street, London, where millions of pounds are turned over daily. The public buildings, such as the Houses of Parliament, the Free Public Library and Art Gallery, which has cost £184,604, and is not yet finished, the Post Office, and the City Hall, are all handsome structures. The warehouses are the best lighted and best arranged buildings for their purpose I have ever seen; and I do not know a street anywhere where so many fine warehouses are so close together as in Flinders Lane. The streets of Melbourne are all laid off at right angles, as the streets are in the newer parts of Glasgow, but there is a wide and a narrow one alternately. The wide one is called, say Flinders Street, and the narrow one Flinders

Lane, or Collins Street, and Little Collins Street, and so on.

The tramway system in the city is much superior to anything of the kind in this country; the trams are all cable lines, and travel nine miles per hour. The fare is threepence for any distance. The river Yarra has been deepened, but not sufficiently to admit the larger class of steamers to come up to the city. It is the filthiest piece of water I ever had the misfortune to be afloat on. The Liffey at the lower part of Dublin is sweet compared to the Yarra, and the Liffey is the dirtiest and worst smelling river in the United Kingdom.

The municipal arrangements of Melbourne are interesting. There are around the city proper fifteen independent boroughs, or Shires, as they are called, each dealing with its own local affairs, but sending representatives to a Metropolitan Board of Works, which deals with matters common to all, such as water, sewage, etc. The educational and charitable institutions of Melbourne are equal to those of any city at home, and the places of instruction and interest, such as the Botanical and Zoological Gardens, are a long way ahead of those of any city at home, except London. The sewage arrangements of the town are wretched, and typhoid fever is common. There is no underground drainage as yet, owing to the larger part of the city being only a few inches above high-water level; but a new system is being gone on with, and the sewage is to be carried several miles into the country, and pumped up on sewage farms.

The gloom of the commercial crisis was beginning to be felt when we arrived. The Federal Bank had suspended payments a little more than a month before, and grave doubts were being expressed as to the stability of the Commercial Bank, which stopped payment three weeks later (April 4th). Reaction, after the excitement of the land boom, seemed to be depressing every one. Prices of land and buildings had collapsed, and with them had gone large fortunes, honestly and industriously acquired, as well as nominal fortunes, represented by bills of various lengths of currency. Great mansion houses of the boomers, which had cost fifty thousand pounds or more, could be had for a hundred pounds or so per annum, and the name of the fashionable suburb in which these were situated had been changed—in a jocular way—from Toorak to Broken Hill. The public revenue, notwithstanding increased duties, was shrinking month by month, and commercial business was diminishing to even a greater extent. But while all outside was in such a depressed condition, in the homes of our friends we found all as cheerful and pleasant as possible. On the evening of our arrival several friends called and spent some time with us; and on Tuesday morning I received intimation that I had been admitted, on the nomination of Sir F. T. Sargood, an honorary member of the Australian Club for a month, of which I took advantage. By the rules of the Club, only members can lunch or dine in it, and no member can introduce a stranger until he has been made an honorary member; and I found the same rules in force in the best clubs in Sydney and Brisbane; but in New Zealand the rules are very much the same as in clubs at home. We spent Tuesday in seeing the city, and lunched and dined with some of our fellow-passengers, with whom we had been on very friendly terms during the voyage.

On Wednesday, after I had called on several of my business friends, we went to lunch with Sir Frederick and Lady Sargood at their residence, Rippon Lea, Elsternwick. The company we met were such as we should have expected to meet at their home; and this being the first colonial mansion we had visited, we were much interested in the house and its surroundings. Without the permission of our host and hostess I do not venture to trespass upon the privacy of their charming home. I cannot, however, help referring to the grounds, extending to about sixty acres, which were to me an interesting study, containing, as they did, specimens of trees and plants from all parts of the southern hemisphere, and not a few from northern latitudes. Water plants luxuriated in artificial ponds, and flowers in abundance enlivened every nook and corner. Two windmills, or wheels, were pumping up water from deep wells into cisterns, from which it was being distributed by fixed pipes in showers all over the garden, and the beautiful green lawn of buffalo grass in front of the mansion, which, with its surroundings of palm houses, fern houses, vineries, and conservatories, formed a picture of an ideal home not easily excelled in any part of the world. The ball-room, a handsome structure detached from the main building, but having a covered way to it, is capable of seating about three hundred persons. The stage at one end had folding doors separating it from a house full of palms and ferns, which form a charming background when the room is used for private theatricals. From a tall tower, built of wood, in the garden we had a fine view of the surrounding country. Having spent a delightful afternoon in most agreeable company, we returned to the city to meet Mr. Butler, Mr. P. P. Fraser, and some other friends whom we had asked to dine with us at our hotel in the evening.

The 16th was very hot. In the forenoon we visited the Botanic Gardens, and spent the afternoon with Mr. and Mrs. Duncan Love at their beautiful residence at Toorak. In the evening we dined with other friends.

On Friday forenoon several old friends we had known at home called, and spent some time with us. In the afternoon we visited the Parliament House, Free Library, Art Gallery, and City Hall with some friends, and were courteously shown through them all. This was the hottest day we had had; the temperature was 130° in the sun, and felt very oppressive to us northeners.

In the evening we dined with the Honourable Robert and Mrs. Reid at their handsome residence, a few miles from Melbourne. Mr. Reid left Scotland when very young, and is now one of the most extensive merchants in the Australian Colonies, a man of whom his native country may be proud, and who is as much esteemed for his private worth as for his eminent business abilities. He is Minister of Defence in the present Government of Victoria, and has since been sent to London on an important mission from the Colony. In his residence we found another house typical of wealthy colonial life. As at Elsternwick, the handsome ball-room formed a feature in the architecture and arrangements of the house; and in the extensive and well-kept gardens we found a refreshing oasis in the midst of fields of dried-up grass and almost leafless trees. Mr. Reid's family we found accomplished musicians, and we enjoyed a most pleasant evening in his hospitable home.

The weather continuing hot, we decided to go to New Zealand, and spend some time again in Melbourne on our return journey; and we left for Dunedin *via* Tasmania, on Saturday the 18th March, in the *Tarawera*, one of the Union Steamship Company's largest boats, a well-appointed vessel, of 1269 tons register, commanded by Captain Sinclair, a native of Orkney, whose amusing stories formed a most enjoyable part of each meal hour.

CHAPTER IV

TASMANIA

Sunday the 19th was another fine day. By 8 P.M. we sighted Tasmania, and during the night sailed along its well-lighted coast towards Hobart, its principal town. About 8 A.M. on Monday we passed Cape Casma, a promontory formed of the most wonderful basaltic columns I have ever seen, compared to which Staffa is quite insignificant. The basaltic formation extended for fourteen miles along the shore, and was of great height. The scenery, as we proceeded up Storm Bay, was very fine; low hills rose on either side, their slopes variegated by the alternate green of wood and pasture; and as we neared the mouth of the river Derwent, on which Hobart is situated, patches of well-cultivated ground added variety to the landscape, and made it a picture of almost unequalled beauty.

The town of Hobart, the capital of Tasmania, is twelve miles up the river, and is beautifully situated, Mount Wellington, rising 4166 feet behind it, forming a fine back-ground; and well-wooded hills, rising from both sides of the river, shelter the orchards and fruit gardens along its banks. Owing, however, to its defective system of drainage, the town is not healthy, typhoid fever being common when the rain comes after the hot season.

We found all the cabs in Hobart were drawn by two horses, and were told that none of the residents would be seen driving in a one-horse conveyance. We engaged one of these at five shillings per hour, and drove out to see the Government House, which had just been vacated by Sir Robert Hamilton, a native of Shetland, whose term of office had expired. It is built on a bend of the river and surrounded by native trees, all of which are evergreens, and the leaves of which hang over the water like a fringe, the effect being most charming. We next went to the Botanic Gardens, which were only in course of formation, and then went some miles into the country for a drive. There we found convicts, guarded by armed warders, making roads,—a more sensible arrangement than keeping them picking oakum, as at home. There are few public buildings of any consequence in Hobart, except the Post Office and the executive offices of the Government. The Parliament House is an insignificant structure near the harbour, and some distance from the other Government buildings.

E

A large number of people from Melbourne and Sydney spend the hot season in Tasmania, where the mean summer heat is only 63°. In winter the mean temperature is 42°, very like the south parts of England. It has a good rainfall, and the vegetation is luxuriant. The island was discovered by Tasman, a Dutch navigator, in 1642, and was named by him Van Dieman's Land, after the Governor of the Dutch East India Islands.

The first British settlement was formed in 1803, and convicts were sent there soon after. The name was changed to Tasmania in 1852, when the transportation of convicts to the island ceased. In 1855 it was granted local representative government; and, like the other Australian Colonies, has its two houses of Parliament, called the House of Assembly and the Legislative Council. The population on 31st December 1891 was 152,619. Of these 55.78 per cent were native born, 21.50 had been born in England and Wales, 7.70 per cent in Ireland, and in Scotland 4.96 per cent. The aborigines of the island have all died out. In 1835 there were 203 of them left, and they were driven into Flinders Island by the white settlers. The native animals are the same as those of Australia.

We left Hobart for Dunedin about 10 P.M.

The berths in the *Tarawera* were small, and all were full. Most of the passengers were sick all the way, and the accommodation on deck was very limited. The sea was rough and the temperature low; and to add to the general discomfort, the cooking and the food were bad. For three days there were no ladies except my two daughters at table. Some good stories of colonial life were told by Captain Sinclair, one of which, at least, I think worth recording. About seventeen years ago, the widow of a hotel-keeper in Melbourne was on her way to New Zealand to visit some friends, when she met on board the steamer a commercial traveller matrimonially inclined, and the two were engaged to be married; but neither the course of true love nor the sea ran smoothly. With a roll of the ship the "commercial" fell down the stair, and broke two of his ribs, and having thus become damaged, the widow withdrew her plighted troth, and engaged herself to the captain, to whom she was married at once by a clergyman on board. But their married life was short; the captain died of heart disease next day, and his wife landed a widow for the second time. She is now the wife of a steward, in one of the New Zealand Shipping Company's steamers; and the damaged "commercial" still survives his disappointment. This story was vouched for by a well-known Dunedin business man, a fellow-passenger of ours.

CHAPTER V

NEW ZEALAND

WE arrived at Campbelltown, or Bluff Harbour, as it is more generally called, early on Friday the 24th March. The town or village is all built of wood, has a good harbour, commodious quays, and a large export trade in frozen meat. It is the nearest port to Invercargill, and the shipping port for the southland district of the Middle Island. The names over the shops were nearly all Scottish. The day was fine, and we spent it on shore while our steamer was discharging cargo. The landscape was very home-like. Gorse and wild brambles grew luxuriantly along the sides of the roads, the same breeds of cattle were feeding on the fields, the grass was of such a green colour as we had not seen since leaving home, and even the sea-weeds by the shore were of much the same forms as at home. But even here a walk of two miles brought us into contact with something new; in a finely-wooded valley not far away we had our first sight of the grand tree ferns of New Zealand. They looked very much like cocoa-nut palms, having a straight bare stem rising up twenty or thirty feet, and an umbrella-like top of drooping leaves. The white tents of a number of men employed in cutting timber gave a picturesque effect to the scene. Having enjoyed a day on shore after our rough sea-passage of 1429 miles from Melbourne, we left in the evening for Port Chalmers, and arrived there at 6.30 A.M. next morning. It is a lovely bay. The hills round it rise rapidly from the water, and are well wooded to their tops. It was here the two ships carrying the first Scottish emigrants to New Zealand landed their brave passengers, among the untrodden ferns, on the 15th of March and 12th of April 1848. They were the outcome of the religious movement which had led to the establishment of the Free Church of Scotland, and, although not persecuted as the Pilgrim Fathers were, they wished to be free to exercise their theological opinions, while they were, I have no doubt, anxious to benefit their families and themselves by settling in a new country where land in abundance could be had for almost nothing. There were 326 of them altogether, and they, unfortunately, landed at the beginning of a most inclement season. For nearly two months they had incessant rain, and, strange to say, they had come without tents, and the women and children had to remain on board the ships while the men did their best to prepare shelters for those dependent on them. A most chilling reception certainly, which only brave hearts could have faced successfully.

Around the beautiful little harbour now rise church steeples and substantial houses, evidently the homes of people to whom the cares of privation are unknown, while crowds of vessels arrive and depart, bringing the rewards, and leaving with the results, of peaceful industries. We had to wait two hours for the tide to rise before we could get up from Port Chalmers to Dunedin, which is situated at the head of a shallow bay, called Otago harbour, through which a channel has been deepened, at a cost of eight hundred thousand pounds.

Dunedin is the Gaelic word for Edinburgh; and the name was suggested to the first settlers by the late William Chambers of "Journal" fame. We arrived there at 10.30 A.M. on Saturday the 25th, and put up at Wain's Hotel, a very comfortable house.

The town of Dunedin is built on a series of ridges running up from the harbour, and the view from the hill above the town is simply charming. The population, including the suburbs, is about 46,000. It has many handsome public and private buildings, including the University, the

City Hall, the High School, and the offices of the Bank of New Zealand, of the Union Steamship Company, and others. The warehouses of Messrs. Sargood, Son, and Ewen, Butterworth Brothers, Ross and Glendinning, Hallenstein Brothers, and others, are all handsome buildings. Princes Street, the principal throughfare of the town, is a handsome street. A statue of Burns adorns an open space in front of the Town Hall; and a handsome monument in memory of the Rev. Dr. Burns, who accompanied the first settlers, and was first minister of the Presbyterian Church, and of Captain Cargill, who was the leader of the same party, has been erected in a place called the Square, in the centre of the town. In Princes Street are the chief retail warehouses, of which Messrs. Brown, Ewing and Co.'s, A. and T. Inglis', and Herbert Haynes and Co.'s, are the largest. While only a small town, Dunedin has the style of a capital city. The day after our arrival being Sunday we felt very much at home: all places of business were closed, and there was an appearance of Sunday rest such as we had not seen since leaving home. We went to a Congregational church in the forenoon, and to the first Presbyterian church in the evening, both of which had large congregations.

For many years after the settlement of Dunedin ecclesiastical authority was supreme, and the

Bible their chief law book; but the Bible is not allowed to be read in any of the schools now, and the Secularist, the progenitor of the state Socialist, is largely in evidence in public affairs.

The 27th I devoted to visiting business friends, and in the evening I renewed the acquaintance of some old friends I had not seen for nearly thirty years, among them Sir Robert Stout, a man who has made a deep impression on the history of his adopted country, and who is at present the most notable of New Zealand politicians. Sir Robert went to Dunedin as a teacher, but studied law afterwards, and is now the leading barrister in the city. He has been Attorney-General, Solicitor-General, and Prime Minister of the Colony. Mr. William Bolt, another old acquaintance, who has been recently appointed an "honourable" member of the upper house of the Legislature, for his political services and ability, called to see us, as did also Mr. William Sinclair of the Colonial Bank, and Mr. Robert Sinclair of the Lands Registry Office, sons of an esteemed friend lately deceased, Mr. Robert Sinclair, merchant, Lerwick.

On Tuesday, after I had attended to some business matters, we had a drive along the hill above the town, and on to the marine suburb called St. Clair, on the sandy beach of which it is said Captain Cook first landed. In the afternoon we were visited at our hotel by some old people who were members of my father-in-law's church for many years before they settled in New Zealand, and who were glad to see my wife for her father's sake, and myself as the present proprietor of the district in which they were born. In the evening we dined with Sir Robert Stout and his amiable lady, where we met a truly Scottish gathering of most pleasant and home-like people.

Thursday forenoon I spent attending to business, and in the afternoon went with Mr. Glendinning, of Ross and Glendinning, to their woollen factory at Roslyn, where ladies' dress goods, hosiery, tweeds, and blankets are manufactured on a large scale. It is the only place where I ever saw so many classes of goods put through from the fleece to the finished articles; and I do not think there is probably another such factory in existence. There are several other woollen factories in New Zealand.

The evening was again spent with friends. Some amusing incidents are related in connection with the early settlement of Dunedin. The first judge was a Mr. Sydney Stephen, who got the appointment through the influence of his brother, the Chief Justice of New South Wales, and a salary of £800 a year when the population scarcely numbered 800. For two years there was not a case to be tried by the judge. At last a case appeared on the list, but in it the judge was the delinquent, and had to appear as defendant—a case of assault. A full bench of magistrates sat to try the judge, and although he pled guilty to the charge, they dismissed the case!

When the judge had so little to do, it will be understood the gaol accommodation needed was not large. The prison was called " Mr. Monson's Establishment," and was a rickety wooden shanty, erected for the confinement of a few male and female topers, with occasionally some runaway sailors, who seem to have formed quite a family party. They were let out by day to work, and in the evening had to present themselves at Mr. Monson's family worship. On Saturday evenings they were sent into town with baskets for next week's provisions, and were told that if they did not return in time they would be *shut out;* and a story is told of one vixen who proved so bad that Mr. Monson would not keep her in the prison.

The Scottish element is no doubt very strong in Otago, and, being the pioneers, they are in possession of the largest portion of the land; but it is a mistake to consider New Zealand an especially Scottish Colony. When the census was taken in 1891 the number who returned themselves as belonging to the Church of England was 253,331, while Presbyterians and other dissenters numbered only 226,971, and Roman Catholics 87,272.

The number of people born in the Colony was 367,000; born in England, 117,000; in Wales, 2214; in Scotland, 57,916; and in Ireland, 47,634.

Nearly all the places of business in New Zealand are closed from the evening of Thursday preceding Good Friday till the following Tuesday.

We had arranged to leave on the morning of Friday the 31st of March for the Lake District, and we started for Lake Wakatipu at 8.10 A.M. The distance to the lower end of the lake is only 175 miles, but the train travelled so slowly that we did not arrive there till 7.30 P.M.

This line of railway passes through the best cultivated part of the Colony. About ten miles from Dunedin we passed through the Taieri Plain, one of the most fertile districts. Shortly afterwards we crossed the river Balclutha, which drains the central lake district, and is said to discharge sixteen times the quantity of water discharged by the river Thames. The Tokomariro district near the river is an excellent district for wheat growing. At a town called Gore, ninety miles from Dunedin, we changed to a private railway company's line, and for nearly seventy miles travelled through the Waimea Plains, a fine grazing country, almost dead level.

Half the so-called stations on this line are only box-like places, having neither station-master nor porter. The guards sell tickets and collect them as they go along. Nearly all the railways in New Zealand are Government property, and ten millions sterling were borrowed for their construction. Only between Dunedin and Invercargill, and Dunedin and Christchurch, do trains run daily each way, the rule being on alternate days, that is, from Dunedin, say to Kingstown on Mondays, Wednesdays, and Fridays, and from Kingstown to Dunedin on the other three days of the week. The average speed of fast trains is twelve miles per hour. When we arrived at Kingstown a small steamer was waiting to take us to Queenstown, about half-way up Lake Wakatipu. The scenery in this part of New Zealand is almost unequalled in any part of the world for grandeur and beauty. A range of mountains called the New Zealand Alps, of which Mount Cook, rising 13,200 feet, is the highest, runs north and south, near the west coast of the Middle Island, and they look grander than the Alps in Europe, owing to their rising more abruptly from the plains. Wakatipu is fifty-eight miles long, and from two to three miles wide, and is surrounded by lofty mountains rising almost perpendicularly from its margin. The day had been fine, and when we went on board the steamer a full moon was shining nearly overhead, in a cloudless sky.

The rugged peaks of the mountains threw their dark shadows on the water, lit by the silvery rays of the moon. Not a sound was heard around us, not a bird could be seen, and even the voices of our fellow-passengers were hushed to a whisper, awed by the majesty of nature around.

We had reached the lake through a gorge between two mountains, and as we steamed up we had Mount Dick, 6020 feet, on our left, and on our right Bayonet Peak, 6417 feet, and before us lay the three black rugged peaks called the Remarkables, rising to a height of 7688 feet, and so steep that their tops are said to be little more than three miles from the lake, between two perpendiculars. They are mountains of lava, and their rugged sides seem to defy nature to clothe them with even the scantiest covering of vegetation. In form they are very like the Coolins in Skye, an extinct crater forming a lake near their base, exactly as Loch Coruisk does in the Coolins. We took three hours to steam to Queenstown, and seemed to be sailing on a silver mirror round which the dark shadows of the mountains formed a frame of ebony. We rounded a point in this vast hollow, and came within sight of the lights of the Alpine-like village of Queenstown, nestling under the shadow of lofty Ben Lomond (5747 feet high), and soon were landed on its tiny pier, and comfortably housed in Echard's Hotel. Saturday the 1st of April was a lovely day, and we left the hotel at 9.15 A.M. for the head of the lake, a distance of thirty-five miles. From Queenstown to the head of the lake the mountains on both sides are covered with vegetation.

We steamed along the northern shore, and the birches and brackens, growing in the hollows of the mountains, gave a picturesque and home-like appearance to the Ben Lomond of the Antipodes. This mountain was named Ben Lomond in 1860 by Duncan M'Ausland, a Scottish shepherd in the employment of Mr. Rees, the first settler in the district. Continuing our voyage, we rounded White's Point, and opened up the magnificent panorama of the upper arm of the lake, the mountain scenery of which is grand in the extreme, and reminded me of the view of the Alps from the hill above Turin. On our left rose the range of mountains called the Humboldts, 8100 feet high, with Mount Alfred farther in front; and in front, to our right, towered Mount Earnslaw, 9200 feet, covered with perpetual snow, its giant glacier, said to be the largest in the world, sparkling in the morning sun. It was a scene never to be forgotten.

Our first landing-place was Kinloch, a township of small dimensions, beautifully situated at the foot of Mount Bonpland, which rises nearly 8000 feet above it. We spent about three-quarters of an hour there, and then crossed to Glenorchy, another village, on a grassy flat backed by the Richardson Mountains. We intended to go to a place called Paradise Flat, and have a nearer view of Mount Earnslaw, and see the famous Rees Gorge, but time would not permit, and we returned by the same steamer to Queenstown. The sail down the lake was delightful, as the evening shades settled down on the hills in colours which we had never seen before, but which are beautifully described by a native poet, Thomas Bracken, who says—

> When all the changeful colours of the eve,
>   Pink, violet, purple fade away,
> With crimson, gold, and amber, but to leave
>   The scene enwrapped in foids of sombre grey.

It was in the neighbourhood of Queenstown that great quantities of gold were found in 1862, which caused so much excitement all over the world, and drew to New Zealand adventurous spirits from all parts of the Empire, and elsewhere. I had an interesting conversation with George Archer, who was the second settler in the district, and one of the first prospectors; and his reminiscences of early life and adventure were most interesting. Mr. Rees, the first settler, is still living in the district, but he has, unfortunately, lost most of his means by the ravages of rabbits and other causes. The 2nd of April was another lovely day; the temperature in the shade was 52°; and being anxious to see the *locale* of the celebrated gold diggings, we drove round by Franktown and Arrowtown, two of the celebrated spots, and home by the Shotover Gorge, but we found neither the diggings nor the landscape interesting. Digging, or rather gold finding, in this district, is now almost confined to dredging up the sand from the bed of the Shotover river, and washing the gold out of it. A few alluvial diggings were being wrought in the neighbourhood, but not to any great extent. There are 600 people in Queenstown; and it is a favourite resort of tourists from all parts of the colonies.

We left for Dunedin at 6.15 A.M. on Monday the 3rd of April, and saw those marvellous shades of light, caused by the rising sun, which I believe is not seen anywhere but in this district of New Zealand. We had seen the sun rising over the cloudless hills along the shores of the Mediterranean, above the mountains of Asia, over the sandy plains near the Red Sea, from the golden fringed horizon of the Indian

Ocean, and above the mountains of Ceylon; but all blended together could not equal the marvellous beauties of light and shade, of subdued rainbow tints, that mingled with the azure blue of the sky overhead, as, on that absolutely calm morning on Lake Wakatipu, the sun rose behind the mountain ranges and drove away the last streaks of dawn from its surface. I cannot satisfactorily describe the scene, but shall never forget it. We landed at Kingstown at 8.15 A.M., and again took twelve hours to travel the hundred and seventy-five miles to Dunedin.

It was Easter Monday, and the train was crowded with people returning home from their holidays; but all were sober and most agreeable.

On Tuesday, the 4th, I called on some of my business friends to say "good-bye"; and in the evening a large number of friends called on us to say "farewell," from whom we parted with feelings of the warmest gratitude for the great kindness we had received during our stay in Dunedin, and our regrets that our time there had been so short.

We left Dunedin for Christchurch by rail at 11 A.M. on the 5th, many of our kind friends meeting us at the station to see us off. We travelled along the coast nearly all the way to Oamaru, the bays and headlands being very much like those on the east coast of Scotland.

Oamaru is a town of 6000 inhabitants, and the second largest in the district of Otago. It has a fine harbour protected by a concrete breakwater, large refrigerating works, a flour mill, and a woollen factory. It is 78 miles from Dunedin, and 152 from Christchurch.

Fifty-two miles nearer Christchurch is Timaru, a town with a population of 4000. It is the seaport for the southern division of Canterbury, and the centre of a rich agricultural district. From this to Christchurch the country is very level and uninteresting. We reached our journey's end at 9 P.M., and put up at Coker's Hotel, which we found a clean, well-kept house. Christchurch is called the Cathedral City of New Zealand. It was founded by the High Church party of the Church of England at the time of the Oxford Tractarian Movement in 1849-1850. That party incorporated a company, called the Canterbury Association, and the first ship sent out by them arrived at Port Cooper on the 16th December 1850. It is the most English-like in architecture of any of the cities of New Zealand, but, being built on level ground, the buildings are not well seen from any place, except the tower of the Cathedral, and not advantageously even there. It has a College, Museum, and Botanic Gardens, but no public buildings of any importance. The new warehouse of Messrs. Sargood,

Son, and Ewen is, next to the Cathedral, the most prominent building in the town.

The river Avon flows through it, and its low, grassy banks are overhung by tall willow-trees, the first of which is said to have been taken from Napoleon's grave at St. Helena. We had a very pleasant outing on the river with our friend Mr. Ballantyne, and saw the first house built in the town, a small dwelling of two rooms. A peculiarity of the district is, that an unlimited supply of water is got by boring down a few feet, and by boring down about 100 feet water at a temperature near freezing-point is had in abundance. The town needs no pipe supply of water, an ample supply being got from wells. The drainage of the town is very indifferent owing to the ground being so flat. Most of the leading business men are Scotsmen. Of the wholesale warehousemen, Mr. Ewen, of Sargood, Son, and Ewen, is a Kincardineshire man; Mr. Ross, of Ross and Glendinning, a Morayshire man; Mr. Beath, of G. L. Beath and Company, a Stirlingshire man; and Mr. Ballantyne, of Ballantyne and Company, is a Selkirkshire man. But Messrs. Strange and Coverdale, the partners of the largest retail house, William Strange and Company, are both Englishmen.

We had fine weather while in Christchurch, and enjoyed our short stay very much. We left for Wellington *via* Lyttleton — which may be called the port or harbour of Christchurch — on the evening of Saturday the 8th April. The distance by rail to Lyttleton is seven miles, and the line passes through a tunnel one and three-quarter miles long (the longest in the Colony), emerging on the shore of a beautiful little bay, surrounded by a semicircle of hills. The population of Lyttleton is about 4000. Nearly all the town is built of wood, and shows well what the early town settlements were like before rebuilding became the order of the day. It has a commodious harbour, and wharves capable of berthing fifty ships at a time, and a good graving dock. We sailed for Wellington at 10 P.M. in an old Clyde steamer called the *Penguin*.

The coast along which we passed during the forenoon of the 9th was very like the coast of Sicily, with fine pasture land near the shore, and snow-clad mountains in the background. About mid-day we crossed Cook Strait, and at 1.15 P.M. landed in Wellington, the capital city of New Zealand, the seat of Government and of the vice-regal court. The population of Wellington is about 33,000. The town is built along the shore of a fine bay, called Port Nicholson, and is backed by high hills, rising very abruptly from the water, giving the town a very picturesque appearance from the sea.

The earth excavated for building stances has been used to reclaim the foreshore, along which extensive quay accommodation has been built, with a depth of twenty-two feet of water at low tide. Nearly all the houses are of wood, as are also the houses of parliament, the vice-regal lodge, and the executive offices of the Government, which last are said to be the largest wooden structures in the world, and are a handsome block of buildings from an architectural point of view. The reason why so many buildings are of wood is the frequency of earthquakes. The drainage of the town is bad, and a new system is being adopted, which it is hoped will improve the public health. There are a number of handsome mercantile buildings in Wellington, and the names of the warehousemen most prominent in Christchurch and Dunedin again crop up, with two or three more added. To Sargood, Son, and Ewen ; Ross and Glendinning ; and Butterworth Bros., are added A. Clark and Sons, W. and A. Macarthur; and Steen, Macky, Logan and Caldwell. The largest retail establishment is that of Messrs. Kirkcaldie and Staines. Here as elsewhere we met with the utmost hospitality. A few hours after we landed we were asked to supper with Mr. and Mrs. Nuttall, and from their hospitable home, perched high up the hillside, we had a fine view of the town stretching along the shores of the bay. We met several old acquaintances in Wellington, one of whom, Mr. Fleming Laurenson, I had not seen for thirty years, and many pleasant recollections of olden times turned up during our short interview. I had only three or four business calls to make in Wellington, and there being few places of interest in the neighbourhood, we decided to leave for Auckland *via* New Plymouth, on Tuesday morning at 6.30. As Monday night was the only one remaining to be spent in Wellington, we had, instead of accepting our friends' invitations, asked them to dine with us, and we spent a very pleasant evening together. The trains on the line from Wellington to New Plymouth run only on two days of the week, so that if we did not leave on Tuesday, we could not get away till Friday, and our time would not permit our staying so long. The distance between these towns is two hundred and fifty-one miles, which we took fifteen and a half hours to travel. The line belongs partly to the Government, and partly to the Manawatu Railway Company. Breakfast was nicely served in a dining-car attached to the train, and the whole journey was a most interesting one. The scenery for the first thirty miles or more was varied and grand, and our interest was increased when we came to a district which was being, in colonial phraseology, "cleared of the bush," *i.e.* forests of magnificent trees, tree ferns, and the undergrowth of creeping and other plants.

The process is a rough and ready one. The trees are first stripped of a portion of their bark all round, which kills them, and then at the end of the dry season the whole district to be cleared is set on fire. We passed near to square miles of burning forest, where the unconsumed trunks of giant trees stood like obelisks marking the spots where men were making a wreck of nature, and raising new homes for themselves. As soon as the burning process is completed, grass seed is sown among the ashes, and in six months sheep will be pasturing on what, twelve months before, was impenetrable forest. Beside the blackened trunks of the trees we saw the white cotton tents or bark-covered huts of the new proprietors, and where the pasture had become green we saw the wooden houses, raised by the strong, healthy settlers, and round them were playing, as free as the lambs, rosy-faced, healthy children whose posterity will, no doubt, be looked upon by future generations of Socialists as descendants of "a bloated landed aristocracy."

It takes many years to clear land for agricultural purposes. The remains of the trees have all to be cut down, and the roots dug up and burned. The expense of doing this is about three pounds per acre.

We dined at a station called Aramoho, a few miles from the town of Wanganui, which was almost the centre of the Maori war which lasted from 1864 to 1870. The railway line runs for some distance along the river Wanganui, which is navigable for vessels of light draught for over a hundred miles. The line passes near the two active burning mountains, Ruaphea and Tongariro, 6458 and 8878 feet high respectively, and also Mount Egmont, 8260 feet high, but it was dark when we were in their neighbourhood, and we did not see them.

It was 10 P.M. when we arrived at New Plymouth, the chief town in the district of Taranaki. It has a population of 3350. We left there by steamer at 10.30 P.M. for Onehunga, a town on a fine bay called Manukau harbour, which bay cuts into the land from the west side of the island, leaving a narrow neck of land only eight miles broad between it and Auckland harbour. It is entered by a narrow channel between a great sandbank and a rocky shore, and is navigable for small vessels only. It was on the sandbank outside this harbour that H.M.S. *Orpheus* was lost when conveying troops to the island to operate against the Maoris in 1869. Onehunga was a military station at one time where a body of pensioners were located to protect Auckland against surprise attacks by the Maoris. We arrived there at 12.30 P.M. on the 12th April, and took the train to Auckland. We had engaged rooms at the Grand Hotel, a building beautifully situated on the top of a hill, and overlooking the town and harbour. The harbour of Auckland is a charming bay, dotted over with islands, and the town is beautifully situated on the rising ground along its shores, while Mount Eden forms a fine background to the picture. Auckland was the capital of New Zealand previous to the union of the provinces in 1876, when the seat of Government was transferred to Wellington, but the Governor's residence is still kept as such, and the Governors even now spend a part of every year in Auckland. The population of Auckland, including the suburbs, is about 52,000, and it has already become the residence of many people who have retired from the more active duties of life. The town has a good supply of water and good drainage. It is the port in New Zealand where the mail steamers between Sydney and San Francisco call. It has many good public and private buildings. Its principal thoroughfare is called "Queen Street," and in it are many good shops and commercial buildings. We spent the afternoon of the day of our arrival in visiting the Botanic Gardens and other places of interest in the town, and in calling on friends, my first call being at the warehouse of Messrs. Archibald Clark and Sons, to which my letters were to be addressed. This firm being my oldest customers in Auckland, I was very pleased to meet the resident partners. Theirs is the oldest established warehouse and manufacturing business in Auckland. The founder of the business, the late Mr. Archibald Clark, was a native of Perthshire, and both he and his sons, who now carry on the business, have done a great deal to make Auckland what it is, while fully sharing in its growing prosperity. The largest warehouse in the town is that of Messrs. W. and A. Macarthur, while those of Messrs. A. Clark and Sons; Sargood, Son, and Ewen; and Macky, Logan, and Co. follow, and are fine buildings, well lighted and arranged for the dispatch of business.

Thursday, the 13th, was a lovely day, and while my wife and daughters were spending the forenoon in visiting friends a little way out of town, I employed my time in looking after business. On the nomination of Mr. Archibald Clark I had been made an honorary member of the Northern Club, and had the pleasure of lunching there with him, and of meeting some old London acquaintances at the same time. In the evening we went to the chrysanthemum show, which was a fair display, but not nearly equal to such shows at home.

On Friday the 14th April, at 9.45 A.M., we left for the hot lake district, that wonderland of the world. For a few miles after leaving Auckland the scenery was interesting, and the land well cultivated. The white painted houses dotted over the landscape gave it a picturesque appearance and an air of cheerful comfort; but on the whole the run to Oxford, the termination of our railway journey, was not particularly enjoyable.

The low-lying country seemed good pasture land, but the higher parts are still covered with the tie-tree and brackens. All the railway time-tables in New Zealand and Australia give the height above sea-level of all stations, and we found the highest point during our day's travel was only 270 feet.

We stopped at a station called Mercer for luncheon, and here we found ourselves in the land of the Maori (the name Maori means simply natives in their language).

Groups of women in dresses of showy prints, smoking pipes, and laughing and behaving very much like a lot of factory girls out for meal time, were hanging about the station. They were all tattooed on the upper lip, and had a tattooed mark like an imperial on the lower. The colour of the marking was a deep blue, and gave them a half fierce, half comical appearance. We saw one or two tattooed old men, but none of the young men tattoo now. They looked a lazy, slouching lot. Mercer is on the Waikato river.

The next place of any interest on this line

of railway is Huntly, where there are several coal mines. Here we saw an old chief, one of those who fought against us in the last Maori war. His face was entirely covered with tattoo marks in well-defined geometrical lines, and he wore a suit of black broadcloth, a wide-awake hat, and Wellington boots, but his name I was unable to learn.

The distance from Auckland to the station called Oxford, where we had to spend the night, is 134 miles, and the time we took to travel it was eight and a half hours. We found the wooden hotel clean and comfortable, and Mr. and Mrs. Rose the best of hosts and hostesses.

There was to be a race meeting in the district next day, and a great many of the betting fraternity ("damned spiders," the landlord called them) were in and about the house, but he kept them in good order, and his house quiet on the whole. The hotel being full, my wife and girls had a double-bedded room, and I a small room to myself in the quarter where the "spiders" were housed. After we had all retired, I overheard one of these gentlemen tell his friend how he had cleared out the pockets of some one in another hotel a few nights before. The *modus operandi*, as he described it, was as follows:—"I put a newspaper under the door, and then with a piece of wire turned the key, which had been left in the lock, so that I could push it in out of the keyhole. I then drew out the paper with the key on it, opened the door from the outside, cleaned the fellow's pockets of fifteen shiners, locked the door again, and pushed the key inside below it." I did not leave the key in the lock of my bedroom door again while I was in New Zealand.

Horse-racing is a very favourite sport all over the Colonies, and the older colonials say the betting connected with it is a curse to the younger generation.

On Saturday the 15th we left Oxford at 7.15 A.M. by coach for Ohinemuti. The coach was the first of its class we had seen. It was a large vehicle like a landau, hung on straps of leather instead of springs, and the jolting as we drove along the rough roads was anything but pleasant; but so lovely was the morning, so bracing the air, so charming the shades of light as the sun rose behind the hills, and so varied the landscape, that we forgot all about the jolting and swinging motions of our conveyance as it rolled up and down hills, over bridges, and through deep cuttings, in the clayey bottoms of which the wheels sank nearly to the bosses. We enjoyed our drive that morning as we had seldom enjoyed a drive before. After two hours' driving the character of the road and scenery changed. The road became more level, and led along a hillside at the bottom of which, lost to view among giant trees, tree ferns, and other vegetation, was the bed of the Waiho river. The gorge through which the river flowed was said to be 850 feet deep, but so filled was it with the overhanging branches of trees growing up its steep sides that it only looked like a mossy dell of no considerable depth, carpeted with greens of many shades and patterns. For the next few miles the road passed along the ridge of a narrow neck of land with deep gorges on both sides, and then on to more level but still rising ground, where we changed horses, and entered on twelve miles of the most romantic road to be found even in New Zealand. It had been cut through a dense forest, the clearing away of the fallen timber having been done by burning as usual.

Tall giants of the forest, stripped of their leaves and blackened by the flames, stood all along the roadside, as if to guard the new way of civilisation; and a few yards farther back the tall *pittosperum* and *totorah* lifted their towering forms high into the sunlight, the intervening spaces being filled with the graceful tree fern and the mop-like cabbage tree. A parasite tree called the rata—which in its earlier stages attaches itself like ivy to a strong neighbour, kills the tree supporting it when it has gained sufficient strength to support itself, and takes its place—grows abundantly in this district, and we were much interested to see it in its various stages of development; and behind the trees, on both sides of the road, hills covered with brackens, etc., rose against the sky-line, and seemed to form a base of support for the arch of ethereal blue overhead. Before coming to the end of this magnificent avenue we had risen to an altitude of a thousand feet, and although mid-day, the air was perceptibly colder than it was in the morning. The road now began to descend, and within a mile or two we cleared the bush, and got our first glimpse of the far-famed hot lake district. From a distance it has nothing striking about its appearance. A lake of moderate size called Rotorua, with a small island in the centre, its shores low, and covered with tie-tree and other dwarf shrubs, small puffs of steam rising all along its margin, a few Maori "whares" by the roadside, and the village of Ohinemuti on a small promontory jutting into the lake, gave us rather an unflattering opinion of the wonderland of which we had heard so much, and had come so far to see. But we found it on closer acquaintance to be one of the most wonderful districts imaginable. A drive of about five miles down to and along the side of the lake brought us to Macrae's Palace Hotel, Ohinemuti, the proprietor of which, an Inverness-shire man, received us kindly, and conducted us to the rooms allotted to us, which opened on the front balcony of the house and commanded an extensive view of the surrounding country. After luncheon we strolled out to investigate the wonders of which we had heard so much. I had read short descriptions of the district by Miss Gordon Cumming, Mr. Sala, and Mr. Froude, and I·was disappointed not to be able to find the hole of which Mr. Froude spoke, where the chief boiled the ambassador sent to him, and where he was afterwards boiled by the ambassador's master; nor the bath in which the Maoris swim with their umbrellas up to keep off the rain; neither could I find the wondrous marble stairways and perfect marble baths referred to; but of other wonders of nature there were enough to interest any one.

A few yards from our hotel was a small lake, about three-quarters by half a mile, which was simply a boiling caldron. A cloud of steam hung over it, and the heat of a stream running out of it was said to be over 200°. By putting down a stick about two feet, a jet of hot vapour could be brought up through the ground, and by putting it down other two feet, hot water would follow its withdrawal. So thin was the crust of the earth over the boiling water below, that it was dangerous to venture near this lake without a guide. The village of Ohinemuti is built on a hillock, near the shore of Lake Rotorua, and the "whares" of the

Maoris are built on the low ground, close by the lake. The district belongs to and is the headquarters of the Arawa tribe. Their houses are of the most miserable type of human dwellings, being built of mud and covered with bark, boards, or old sacks laid over sticks, the floors of bare earth, and each of one apartment only. A large number of hot springs bubble up close by the Maori dwellings, and they have lined a space round the opening of one of these with boards, and made it the chief cooking pot of the village. When they want to cook eggs or potatoes, they put them in a net and suspend them in the hot water, and their fish, beef, and bacon are cooked in the same way. We saw them bringing tea-kettles filled with cold water, and placing them in the hot springs to boil. A most extraordinary thing is that hot and cold springs are found within a few yards of each other. The temperature of Lake Rotorua is about 130°. A few miles from Ohinemuti is a place called Whakarewarewa, and there the hot springs take the form of geysers, spouting their steaming fluid up to a height of from thirty to sixty feet. The water is heavily charged with sulphur and silica, the deposits of which have formed small pink and white terraces. But what surprised us most at this place was the terrible rumbling and thudding noises beneath our feet, as if a battle-ground of demons was situated below. When the great geyser had sent up its spout of boiling water for a few moments, the noises below ceased, as if they had exhausted themselves, the spouting up ceased also for a time, and then the same great struggle took place again, till relieved by another upheaval of the boiling liquid. Within a few yards of this great geyser opening, hot springs and cold springs were pouring their waters into the almost boiling river below; and within another short distance, great openings were pouring out streams of boiling mud. The sounds and sights made us stand aghast; but close by, in pools of tepid water, Maori youths and children were enjoying their baths amid the terrible turmoil of nature; and old women were sitting outside their houses on flat stones warmed by the genial heat from the ground, smoking their pipes, and I presume discussing their local gossip. The smell of sulphur and other chemical substances thrown off by these springs was very disagreeable, and we were glad to get away from their neighbourhood; but we had not yet seen the most appalling of these wonders of nature.

Next day we drove twelve miles to a place called Tikiteri, a valley about two miles by one, in which are centred all the peculiarities of the hot lake district. The bottom of the valley is over 1000 feet above sea-level, and it is surrounded by high hills. The first thing which arrested our attention when we entered the valley was a great opening in the side of the hill facing us, from which immense volumes of steaming hot water were being thrown, as if some gigantic pump were at work below the ground; and as the water fell back into the steaming orifice, it sounded as if it would suck into the regions below anything coming near it. Near the centre of the valley the scene around was simply indescribable. Sulphur fumes hung over the place like a fog, and the hissing noise made by jets of steam, the gurgling noises made by dozens of openings vomiting out boiling mud, streams of sulphurous liquid, of water permeated with alum and silicate, and of oily and unknown compounds, gave us the impression of all the infernal elements let loose; and we did not feel at all comfortable when taken in hand by the guide, Pat Macoran, an Irishman, married to a hunch-backed Maori woman, the proprietrix of the district, and by him led over very crusty bridges formed of sulphur and pumice from the regions below. These bridges or footpaths were merely hardened crusts on the surface of the boiling sulphur pools beneath them. We followed Pat singly, and at some distance from each other, so as not to overweight these unsubstantial structures. On one side of the track, as we crossed this valley of desolation, was a small lake of clear boiling water, and on the other a lake of some compound from which rose sulphur-laden steam, which made the air almost unbreathable unless when the breeze swept the fumes away. Farther on, springs of cool mineral waters bubbled up as peacefully as if miles away from the turmoil around them, and were flowing through pools, called baths, much frequented by people suffering from diseases of the skin and rheumatism. A bridge of almost pure sulphur spanned a space between two boiling pools, one of black mud, the other of a substance called "oil," from both of which odours of the most disagreeable character arose. This bridge, of almost golden colour, was called "Hell's gate," and as I stood behind the guide, watching the boiling compounds, two lines of Dante's came forcibly to my mind, viz.—

> So not by force of fire, but art divine,
> Boiled here a glutinous thick mass,

and I almost expected to see the heads of the rebellious appear above the surface.

Our exit from the valley was by a footpath formed of hardened mud, and we felt as if we were escaping from Purgatory.

The Maori mode of cooking at Tikiteri was different to that at Ohinemuti. At Tikiteri a hole was bored a foot or two into the ground, up through which steam rushed, and the natives had a square frame of wood, with a lid on it, placed over the opening, and a few bracken leaves laid in the bottom of the frame to place their food on, which was then stewed by the steam from below. A stream of hot water flows from this valley into Lake Rotorua. There are no trees of any great size in this district, but it is covered with the bush called tie-tree, which in the spring flowers abundantly, giving the district the appearance of a vast flower garden. On our way back we passed a place called Sulphur Point, a field of solid sulphur several acres in extent, with a depth of several yards. A small factory was at work preparing flour sulphur for the Auckland market; and when, within a year or thereby, the railway is completed to Ohinemuti, there should be a considerable trade done in that article. The Government have built a sanatorium, for the treatment of various diseases, beside some of the most noted springs; and so famous have the cures become, that people suffering from sciatica, gout, etc., visit the sanatorium from all parts of Australia, and even India. The Maoris of Ohinemuti have a building, called by them their "public hall," in which they receive and entertain distinguished strangers from other tribes. The front of it is covered with figures of the most grotesque description, the faces having shells inserted for eyes, ears, and mouths.

The natives seemed to have selected the hottest spots for their "whares," and to be entirely indifferent to the fact that only a few feet of uncertain crust existed between them and the steaming hot regions below. The population of Ohinemuti is about 300, mostly Maoris.

I expected to be able to procure many curiosities of native manufacture, but I found the only genuine articles to be had were a few stone axes and some baskets, of which I bought specimens. We left Ohinemuti at mid-day for Oxford, by the same coach which took us there, and arrived at the latter place at 6.30 P.M. on the 17th. The hotel was again full, but the races were over, and the "spiders" gone.

We left Oxford at 6.30 A.M., and arrived at Auckland at 2.30 P.M. on the 18th. The afternoon was wet, and we spent it indoors writing letters for home.

Wednesday the 19th was fine. I spent the forenoon making business calls; and at 12.30 P.M. we went with some friends to Devonport, on the north side of the harbour, and lunched with Professor Brown, of University College, at his beautiful English-like residence, and had a most enjoyable drive with him round Lake Takapuna in the afternoon.

We had to leave our kind host at 5.30 P.M. for Auckland, to fulfil an evening engagement with other friends, having added another most enjoyable afternoon to our stay in New Zealand.

Thursday forenoon was spent in making calls. I lunched again at the Northern Club with Mr. M'Millan (of W. and A. Macarthur), and at two o'clock Mr. Finlayson (of Sargood, Son, and Ewen) called at the hotel for us, and drove us out to his house for afternoon tea, and thence to the residence of an old Glasgow friend, Mr. George M'Farlane, now of Inversloy, Onehunga, where we dined and spent the evening.

I had paid my last business visits in the forenoon, and the impressions I had formed of the business men of New Zealand were, that they combined order with activity, and possessed the energy of youth with the experience of their fathers; and I found all of them, native and imported, had a very high opinion of their country. Some had come to the Colony in search of health, and having renewed their youth, seemed determined to make their renovated lives a success. In business they are keen, while courteous and straightforward.

Friday, the 21st, was to be our last day in New Zealand. We had booked our passages to Sydney in the San Francisco mail steamer, and made arrangements to spend the afternoon with friends; but the steamer arrived about six hours before her usual time, and we had to go on board at 2 P.M.

We rose early in the morning and had a drive to the top of Mount Eden, from which we had a charming view of the surrounding country. The district round Auckland is entirely volcanic in its origin, and it is said that thirty extinct craters can be seen from the top of Mount Eden, which is itself one. After a delightful drive we returned to our hotel, and having sent our luggage on board the steamer, called on several friends to say good-bye. Our tour in New Zealand had been a most interesting and enjoyable one. We had had perfect health and most delightful weather. We had met many old friends and made many new ones. We had seen the process of converting impenetrable forests into smiling fields, and the march of progress in social life from bark-covered huts to large universities. We had seen what we considered a model country in its climate, laws, and social arrangements, and we had found contentment and plenty everywhere. I had known many of its pioneer business men at home, and had had much pleasure in meeting many whose names were familiar in my everyday business life. My strong sympathy with the spirit of enterprise which makes men and women colonists, and admiration for the mental and physical vigour which enables them to face all the difficulties connected with life in a new country, and carve out for themselves fortunes under new conditions and amid new associations, had been much gratified by what I had seen. We had learned something of the history, native population, and natural resources of the country. Its magnificent mountain scenery, lovely lakes, charming landscapes, and wonderful objects of nature had made a lasting impression on our minds ; and the kindness and hospitality we had met with had made us feel under obligations we can never repay to our kind friends ; and it was with no ordinary feelings of regret that we stood on the deck of the steamer as the shades of evening closed around us and hid from our view, most probably for ever, the shores of the land in which we had spent such a delightful holiday.

We found the steamer *Alameda*, on which we embarked for Sydney, an excellent vessel of high speed and good passenger accommodation, and Captain Morse and his officers all we could wish as seamen and gentlemen.

While the name of New Zealand was a familiar household word, I found, when I intended to go there, that I could get very little information, beyond ordinary commercial knowledge, regarding it, and I have therefore thought that the following notes, taken mostly from official documents, may be in part new and of some interest to my friends for whom this little volume is intended.

The first authentic account of the discovery of

New Zealand is given by Abel Jansen Tasman, who sailed from Batavia in August 1642. After having visited Mauritius and discovered Tasmania, called by him Van Dieman's Land in honour of the governor of the Dutch possessions in the East Indies, he sailed in an easterly direction, and on the 13th of December in that year sighted the west coast of the middle island.

It has, however, been assumed that the land described by Juan Fernandez, who sailed from the west coast of South America in 1576, was New Zealand.

William Bleau, of Amsterdam, who died in 1638, published a famous atlas in which it appears as Zealandia Nova. There is no record of any visit to New Zealand from Tasman's departure to that of Captain Cook in 1769.

In 1793 it was visited by Lieutenant Hanson on behalf of the New South Wales Government, and continuous intercourse was kept up between it and New South Wales, to which, in 1840, it was formally annexed and put under its laws; but in 1841 it was proclaimed a separate Colony, with Captain Hobson as Governor.

The first attempt at its colonisation was made in 1825 by a company formed in London; but the attempt was a failure, owing to the savage character of the natives.

In the meantime a number of white men from

whaling ships, which were in the habit of refitting in the Bay of Islands, married native women and settled in different parts of the country. In 1838 a new company, called the New Zealand Colonisation Company, was founded to establish settlements on systematical principles, and Colonel W. Wakefield was despatched by that Company in 1839 to purchase land from the natives. He arrived in Cook's Strait in August of the same year, and selected the shore of Port Nicholson as the site of the first settlement; and on the 22nd of June 1840 the first body of emigrants arrived and founded the town of Wellington. About the same time a treaty was entered into between Captain Hobson and the natives, by which the latter ceded to the Queen the sovereignty over the islands, while they retained all territorial rights. The text of the treaty was briefly as follows:—" The Maori chiefs to cede to the Queen for ever the right of government over the whole country. Second, the Queen to confirm to the Maoris their full rights over all their properties, but they cede to the Queen the right to purchase such land as they are willing to sell at a price agreed upon between them and an officer of her Majesty. Third, in consideration of the above, the Queen to protect all her Maori subjects and grant them the same rights and privileges as if they were Englishmen."

The settlements at Nelson and New Plymouth were founded in 1841. The Imperial Government granted representative institutions to the Colony in 1852, and provided for the constitution of a General Assembly for the whole Colony, consisting of a Legislative Council, the members of which were to be nominated by the Governor, and an elective House of Representatives. The first session of the General Assembly was opened on the 27th day of May, but the executive were not responsible to Parliament. The first Ministry under a system of responsible government were appointed in 1856. The area of the Colony is about one-seventh less than that of Great Britain and Ireland together.

It may not be out of place to refer here to the native population. The traditions of the Maoris themselves prove that they were not originally natives of New Zealand, though where they came from is not known; but it is most likely that they came from one of the Navigator Islands during the fifteenth century. According to their traditions they were under the command of a chief called Ngahue, and numbered, when they arrived in New Zealand, four or five hundred.

When Captain Cook visited the islands in 1769 he estimated the population at 90,000. In 1891 they numbered 41,993. From 1886, when they were first numbered, to 1891 they had rather increased in number. There is a low birth-rate among them, owing, it is said, to the widespread immorality among the younger females before marriage, and a high death-rate owing to the want of ordinary care and cleanliness. As yet they have only partially adopted the costume and habits of civilised life. It is no uncommon thing for ten or a dozen of them to sleep in one whare or hovel, with every opening closed, and then get up and go outside on a cold morning with only a rug around them, and sit smoking their pipes for hours, thus causing diseases of the respiratory organs, from which they suffer much. They were cannibals when first known to Europeans, and remained so until recently.

They are a large-boned, well-developed race; but their bodies are longer and their limbs shorter in proportion than those of Europeans, which gives them a dragging gait. But they are said to be agile and to bear fatigue well. Their skin is a sienna brown colour. The women are not so good looking as the men, which may be accounted for by their doing all the work, which makes them look old and haggard-like even when young.

They have never possessed any skill in manufacturing fabrics, the only cloth they ever made being a kind of matting from native flax. They never were workers in metals. Their war implements were spears pointed with bones, and clubs of wood or stone. Their stone axes are made of a hard greenstone, and well shaped. With the exception of one tribe they are all nominally Christians now, and like other Christians, are divided into several sects, those of the Church of England and the Roman Catholics being the largest. Their primitive religion is somewhat difficult to define. They believed in a future state, but not in an Omnipotent Being. Their world to come was a kind of Valhalla. They believed strongly in sorcery and witchcraft. The chiefs and priests divided the spiritual authority between them; but the priests were the scholars of the tribes, and performed special functions. To them was entrusted the peculiar business of tatooing, and they had the power of casting the spell of Tapu, which made anything sacred over which it was cast, from a chief down to a canoe, or a field of potatoes. The first missionary who settled among them was the Rev. Mr. Marsden, an Episcopalian; and he was labouring very successfully when the Wesleyans began a mission; and a few years later the Roman Catholics also; and the Maoris came to the conclusion that if the learned white men could not agree among themselves which was the right and the best way to go to heaven, how could they be expected to know which to choose, and their conversion to Christianity was thereby much retarded. Their intellects are fairly quick, though not deep. Their native system of government was very interesting. They were divided into eighteen nations, the nations were divided into tribes, and the tribes into lodges. The principal chief governed like a modern king, but in important matters he could not act without the assent of the whole body of the people, obtained through the chiefs of nations and tribes. Now they are represented by two members in the Upper, and four in the Lower House of the New Zealand Parliament; and these are said to be able to hold their own in debate with their white compeers, and to take an intelligent interest in the proceedings of both Houses, particularly in matters affecting their race and interests. Many of them have large incomes from lands leased to the Government and private individuals. No white man can now acquire land from the Maoris without the sanction of the Government Land Court. Their lands are held in common by the individuals forming the different tribes, and no sale can be made without the consent of all concerned. There was a Land Court sitting at Ohinemuti when we were there, and a Maori barrister, who was acting as agent for the natives, was living in the same hotel. He was a quiet, agreeable man, and quite *au fait* in the forms of civilised life. Their hostility to Europeans may be regarded as a thing of the past, although some of the tribes have not fully emerged from the state of isolation in which they had hedged themselves. They were a brave and warlike race. There was a peculiar code of honour among the tribes, that when they intended to attack each other, they sent word that they intended to do so; and when at war with the whites in 1867, they twice allowed our men to get supplies when they could have prevented them, remarking, "White men can't fight without grub!" They own more than ten million acres of land, of which in 1891 they had under crops 75,883 acres; and they owned 262,763 sheep and 42,912 cattle, besides horses, pigs, etc. The Maori population in 1891 was over 47,000, and there were seventy-four schools for their children, which cost the Colony £17,566, the attendance being 3778. At the same time there were 251 white men married to native women, but only 91 of their children attended Maori schools, the others going with the children of the Europeans.

I have already given the nationality and religious denominations of the white population of New Zealand, but a few other facts regarding them may be interesting. They are divided into 336,174 males and 290,484 females. There are 105 males for every hundred females of marriageable age. In the census returns for 1891 there is a table of those called "bread-winners."

Of these 15,821 were professional, 24,928 domestic, 43,196 commercial, 70,521 industrial, 90,546 agricultural, and 7751 indefinite, and their dependents, non-workers, numbered 373,895. The death-rate in the Colony in 1892 was 10.06 per thousand, while in England it was 17.9, in Scotland 18.0, and in Ireland 17.5. The deaths numbered 5994, of which 524 were caused by phthisis, and of these deaths 209 were of natives. Typhoid fever and diphtheria caused 175 deaths, chiefly due to want of proper sanitary arrangements in the larger towns. There were 450 deaths from accidents. There were 2238 lunatics, 1346 men and 892 women, in the Colony in 1891. In the same year there were convicted before the criminal courts 811 English, 633 Irish, 309 Scottish, and 316 native-born individuals. The divorces were 7.85 for every thousand marriages, as against 1.88 in Britain. About $3\frac{1}{2}$ per cent of the population are employed in manufacturing, against $24\frac{1}{2}$ per cent in Britain. Flax mills employ over 3000 people, and the estimated annual value of their productions is £234,266. Woollen mills employ 1175, and their output is valued at £279,175. Sawmills employ 3266, and send out material of the annual value of £832,959. For the population the printing industry is a very large one, employing 2569 people, and producing an output of the value of

£354,559. Clothing and hat factories employ 3345 individuals, and turn out goods to the value of £591,943 per annum; and most other industries are represented on the list of their home productions, showing that those who have taken possession of the Colony have brought with them as good a knowledge of other useful arts as of agriculture.

Wages vary in different parts of the Colony, but the following, which I have extracted from the returns made to the Government in 1891, may be taken as a fair average:—

Farm labourers	12s. to 15s.	per week with board.	
Ploughmen	15s. to 20s.	,,	,,
Female domestics	8s. to 12s.	,,	.,
Female cooks	12s. to 20s.	,,	,,

while shop assistants receive only 4s. to 8s. per day, and have to pay 15s. to 20s. per week for board.

Stock keepers and shepherds are paid £30 to £60 per annum with board; masons, 8s. to 10s. per day; carpenters, 6s. to 8s.; plasterers, 7s. to 8s.; bricklayers, 7s. to 8s.; smiths, 8s. to 9s.; plumbers, 9s. to 11s.; painters, 8s.; and labourers, 5s. to 8s.

A house of two rooms costs about 12s., and of three rooms 14s. per week.

The average price of beef is 5d.; mutton, 4d.; lamb, 5d.; pork, 4d.; and salt butter, 8½d. per lb.

A 4-lb. loaf costs 7d.; eggs, 1s. per dozen; sugar, 3d. per lb.; milk, 3d. per quart; cheese, 4½d. per lb.; tea, 2s. 6d., and coffee, 1s. 8d. per lb.; whisky is sold for 4s. 6d. per bottle, and beer, 1s. 2d. per quart, or 6d. per glass. The quantity of tea consumed is about 118 ounces per head of the population, as against 90 ounces per head in Britain, but the consumpt of spirits is about 11 per cent less; of wine only about one-half, and of beer only one-third, the quantity per head consumed at home.

By the Land Act of 1892, lands yet in possession of the Government are sold on the following terms: first, for cash; second, occupation with right of purchase; third, lease in perpetuity. The price for first class rural land is 20s. to 25s. per acre, and for second class 10s. to 15s. per acre. Lands of special value are sold by auction. A cash purchaser is given a certificate of occupation, authorising him to hold and occupy the land, but before a Crown charter is issued to him, he must expend, on substantial improvements of a permanent character, a sum equal to 20s. on first, and 10s. per acre on second class land, but he is allowed seven years in which to do this. For occupation with a right of purchase, an occupation license is issued for a term of twenty-five years, subject to an annual payment equal to five per cent on the cash price of the land, payable half yearly. After two years the holder has the option of purchasing the freehold of the land for cash or of exchanging the license for a lease in perpetuity, or he may continue to the end of his term of license. The lease called "in perpetuity" is for 999 years, and the rent 4 per cent on the cash value at the time of purchase. There are various provisions in regard to residence and improvements, for which I must refer my readers to the Act, or to Mr. Vincent Pyke's able treatise on it.

The cost of clearing bush land is about 30s. per acre for grazing purposes, but for farming it may cost as much as 60s. per acre, and the capital required to work a farm is from 40s. to 60s. per acre. Most of the Crown lands not yet taken up are not easy of access, but the country is being opened up by roads. Land already under cultivation costs from £3 to £10 per acre. Men with a small capital, going to New Zealand, should always work for wages for a year or two, till they learn how farming or business is done, and come to understand how best to invest their money. For farmers with £500 to £1000 of capital the North Island is best. Farming is now very remunerative to men who know it well. The greatest extent of land that can be applied for by any one applicant is 640 acres of first class, or 2000 acres of second class land.

The public debt of the Colony, at the end of 1892, amounted to £38,713,068; but it must be remembered that it has been mostly invested in remunerative undertakings, and not spent for war purposes, as most of the public debts in Europe have been. Of the money borrowed by the Government, £14,104,093 has been invested in railways, £606,648 in telegraphs, £4,478,481 in roads, bridges, and harbours, £1,780,785 in public buildings; and for water supplies and other public works the Government have spent £6,007,775. Previous to 1870 a debt of £9,724,723 had been incurred, but no official statement is given as to how that money was expended. The debts of local bodies amount to £6,668,889, and the mortgages on property publicly recorded to £30,502,231, and other private indebtedness has been estimated at £17,000,000, whereas lands, public and private, and other property of all classes are valued at £218,033,963. But this value is purely hypothetical, and varies according to the basis on which it is calculated. The railways paid 2.95 per cent on their cost in 1890-91, the last year for which I have been able to obtain returns.

The total imports for 1892 were £6,943,056, of which £4,767,369 came direct from the United Kingdom, £1,071,563 from Australia, largely by trans-shipment, £120,723 came from continental

Europe, and £381,651 from America. The duty collected on the imports amounted to £1,654,064. The value of imports into Auckland was £1,124,308; Wellington, £1,124,795; Lyttleton (for Christchurch), £788,223; Dunedin, £1,109,165; and Napier £221,499. The total exports were £9,490,420, of which there went direct to the United Kingdom £7,483,618, to Australia £1,338,167, America £524,196, and to continental Europe £9701. The shipments from Auckland were £1,642,686; from Wellington, £1,527,186; from Lyttleton, £1,206,080; from Dunedin, £1,618,567; and from Napier, £1,152,011.

Of the exports, wool was the most valuable, realising £4,313,307; frozen meat, of the value of £1,194,724, being next. Under the heading of animal products the value amounted to £6,271,280, and under the heading of agricultural products the amount was £1,035,637, and of minerals £1,044,945. The value of timber was £100,000, and of Kauri gum £517,678. This latter article is formed of the turpentine that had exuded from Kauri trees, when there were forests of them where they have now ceased to exist. It is found a little under the surface of the ground, and is used for making fine varnishes. It is worth at present £8 to £10 sterling per cwt.

The value of the gold produced in New

Zealand, up to 1892, was £48,387,861, but how much British gold had been sunk in worthless mines is not tabulated. When gold mines have been wrought out, and are what is called "Deadheads," their past output is carefully stated in glowingly-worded prospectuses, and they are sold in London for more gold than they have ever produced.

There were no fourfooted animals in New Zealand when Captain Cook visited it in 1769, except a few dogs and rats. In 1891 there were 17,865,423 sheep, 788,919 cattle, 211,040 horses, and 222,553 pigs. Deer were introduced into the Middle Island by John A. Ewen, Esq., of Sargood, Son, and Ewen, and there are now herds of them in the forests, and some splendid specimen heads were sent home to Mr. Ewen a few months ago. Mr. Ewen took an active part in introducing trout, which are now abundant in several of the rivers, and grow to an enormous size. He has also succeeded in introducing lobsters into New Zealand waters, which are likely to thrive and multiply, as all creatures sent from home have done, man not excepted.

CHAPTER VI

SYDNEY

OUR voyage from Auckland to Sydney was a very pleasant one. There were only about thirty passengers in the *Alameda*, but they were a very agreeable company. We arrived at the entrance to Port Jackson, which is less than a mile wide, and lies between two high headlands, at 9 A.M. on the 25th of April, and an hour later landed at Woolloomoolloo wharf, and drove to the Australia Hotel, where we had engaged rooms. This hotel we considered the best we had seen south of the line. It is a handsome building, said to have cost £240,000, and is well conducted in every way. Sydney Harbour we found to be a very charming bay, more like an inland lake than an arm of the sea; but, as a sheet of water, it is not equal to Loch Lomond. There are many small islands in it covered with luxuriant vegetation, among which are built handsome villas; and along its beautiful shores are many fine residences, all white painted and surrounded by lovely gardens. The city of

Sydney is very home-like in its architecture, but more continental in its style than any of the other Australian towns. The streets are narrower and shorter than those of Melbourne; but Pitt Street, George Street, and York Street, are all very handsome thoroughfares.

The offices of the Lands Department, the Post Office, and the City Hall (in which is the largest organ in the world, said to have cost £15,000), are all splendid specimens of modern architecture, as are also many bank and commercial buildings. The Botanic Gardens, both as regards situation and the collection of plants, trees, etc., are unequalled by any in the Australian Colonies; and as a piece of landscape gardening, I have not seen anything to surpass them except at Monte Carlo. Sydney has also a good collection of pictures for a modern city, and an interesting museum. The tramways are dirty road trains, consisting of large railway carriages, drawn by small locomotives. The fares are about 1½d. per mile. The harbour of Sydney is strongly fortified, and guarded by a regular militia. The best view of the harbour is from near the lighthouse on the south head; and the drive to it is a very fine one.

We had several trips on the harbour steamers, to the north shore, to Paramatta, and elsewhere, all of which were very enjoyable. Botany Bay is eight miles from Sydney by steam tram. We did not find anything in that district to interest us. The population of Sydney and suburbs in 1891 was 443,492, and the rental £6,013,697, and of Melbourne, 490,896, and £6,815,315 respectively; while the rental of Glasgow and suburbs, with nearly the population of both, was under £5,000,000, showing how much more costly houses and shops are in Australia than at home. The city of Sydney has a municipal debt of £3,306,649 for water-supply, £1,447,287 for sewage, £598,508 for public parks, and £710,000 for other purposes. Wages are about the same as are paid in New Zealand, and the working day is eight hours.

There was an air of slowness about the whole business of the city which I did not find in any other of the Australian towns; but whether this is habitual, or was caused by the depression in connection with the bank failures, I am unable to say. The warehouses, with the exception of that of W. Gardner and Co., are not so large as those in Melbourne, but they are equally well arranged and lighted; and those of Henry Bull and Co., Robert Reid and Co., and W. and A. Macarthur, are handsome buildings; and in the extensive warehouse of Anthony Hordern and Sons is done the largest retail trade of any firm in the southern hemisphere. Other fine retail warehouses are those of Farmer and Co., E. Way and Co., and

David Jones and Co. We spent from Tuesday forenoon to Saturday afternoon in Sydney, and then I left for Brisbane by steamer, leaving my wife and daughters to spend a few days with friends.

CHAPTER VII

QUEENSLAND

THE distance between Sydney and Brisbane by sea is 500 miles. The sail along the coast was very uninteresting, the shores being low and sandy, and only near the mouths of the principal rivers was there any appearance of cultivation.

. The range of mountains which run north and south near the coast is not of any great height, all being below the snow line, and consequently the rivers are small, but the Richmond is navigable for small craft for sixty miles, the Clarence for sixty-two miles, and the Maclay and Hawkesbury for shorter distances. When we arrived at the mouth of the river Brisbane, we found that the floods of February had so silted up the channel that we had to go sixteen miles up to the town of Brisbane in a barge. The river, at the part where the town is built, is shaped almost like an S, and the highest point of the ground on which the town stands is only fifty feet above high-water mark. The whole of the rain which caused the disastrous flood fell within twenty miles of the town, and the fall was thirty-nine inches in twenty-four hours. The great damage done by the flood was not apparent to a stranger, when I was there, except in the ruin of bridges, and of some unoccupied houses, but the damage was said to be over two millions sterling to private property. The Gresham Hotel, in which I stayed, was flooded to within a few inches of the first floor, and the residents were supplied with food from boats at the first floor windows. The warehouses of Messrs. D. L. Brown and Co., and Scott, Dawson, and Stewart, were flooded to the first floors, and these firms had a large amount of damage done to their stocks. I saw a photo showing Messrs. Brown's people in a steam-launch opposite their first floor windows. These floods occur periodically, but no special provision for such contingencies seems to be made in any of the buildings. The day I arrived in Brisbane was a holiday in celebration of the passing of the Act establishing "an eight hours' day," and there were processions of all the different trades, followed by races and other amusements, filling up the day.

This was the only opportunity I had in the Colonies of seeing large bodies of working men together, and the physique of the Brisbane men was certainly far above the average in such gatherings at home. In the afternoon I went to the races; and while sobriety and order prevailed, it was a saddening sight to see women, with children in their arms, staking their half-crowns and their half-sovereigns on their favourite horses, and as excited over the events as if fortunes were at stake. All classes of people were represented on the course, and money was changing hands freely. So popular are horse-races in the Colonies that book-makers are regarded as men of considerable social standing.

The town of Brisbane is one of the most modern capitals, and the Government offices are only in course of construction. They will be handsome, but not extravagant buildings when finished. There are several handsome commercial buildings in the town, the finest being that of D. L. Brown and Co., which is also the largest dry-goods warehouse in the Colonies.

The two largest retail establishments are those of Grimes and Petty, and Finney, Isles, and Co.

I spent the evening with some friends, and next forenoon called on my customers, most of whom I had not seen before. It is very pleasant to meet business men who have all their time occupied with local affairs, but who have many pleasant associations with, and recollections of the homes of their early days, which they like to call to memory, with even a stranger who has some knowledge of the places of their nativity and the old folks at home.

Queensland has 2406 miles of railway, constructed at a cost of £16,143,174, and at the head of this great department, as chief Government Commissioner, is Mr. John Matheson, lately superintendent of the Glasgow and South-Western Railway line, an old friend, with whom I spent most of an afternoon, pleased to find him in excellent health and his usual good spirits. The railway system in Queensland is rapidly developing its mineral and natural resources, and the future prospects of that Colony are second to none on the Australian Continent. The population of the Colony, which in 1860 was only 28,056, is now nearly 400,000, and the exports in 1891 amounted to £7,415,431, the imports being £4,941,765. The value of wool exported in that year was £3,453,548; of frozen meat, £240,000; of sugar, £630,000; and of gold, £1,951,563. Gold is found in nearly every district of Queensland, the production to the end of 1891 being £28,052,199.

In 1891, the value of silver raised was £21,879; of tin, £116,387; of coal, £128,198; of bismuth, £11,070; opals, £10,000; and antimony, £3625.

The pastoral industry of the Colony is a very large one.

At the end of 1891 the area of pastoral

holdings was 438,165 square miles, and the annual value £310,812. The number of sheep was 20,289,633; of cattle, 6,192,759; of horses, 399,364; and of pigs, 122,672. At the beginning of 1892 there were sixty-eight sugar mills producing 51,219 tons of sugar per annum; and connected with them were nine rum distilleries, yielding 192,051 gallons of spirits yearly.

The production of wine in 1891 was 168,526 gallons.

The number of oranges grown in the Colony in 1892 was 1,090,804 dozen; of bananas, 11,644,769 dozen; and of pine-apples, 543,415 dozen.

Wheat, maize, barley, potatoes, and tobacco grow abundantly. In 1891 the Colony exported 682,252 pounds of arrowroot.

The revenue for the year ending 30th June 1892 was £3,473,716, and the expenditure £3,625,280. Education costs the Colony over £200,000 per annum, and is secular and free. The death-rate in 1892 was 13 per thousand per annum. A general election was going on when I was in Brisbane, and feeling between the trade unions and all other sections of the community ran very high, and, while kept under police control, seemed more intensely bitter than anything I have ever seen at home. If the man who said "the classes were against the masses" in this country, could have seen the effect of the animosity between the two sections of the people in Brisbane he must have wished that sentence had never been uttered. The recent strikes had crippled trade in the Colony, and the bank failures had added to the general depression, causing a great deal of want of employment and distress. The Government had been asked by the unemployed to start relief works and state-aided village settlements, but they were averse to both on principle. They had, however, opened labour bureaux, and kept themselves in communication with all parts of the country, and assisted men to reach places where work was to be had. The inquiry that was made into the circumstances of all applicants for relief disclosed a great deal of imposture, many applicants having considerable property. Many men in the large towns had, on pretence of going to the country to secure work, abandoned their wives and families, and these had to be provided for by the Government or private charity. But I am glad to know that since I was there trade has improved, and employment become more abundant. Wishing to see the country inland, I decided to go back to Sydney by rail, and left Brisbane at 6.20 P.M. on Wednesday, 3rd May. The distance between these towns is 739 miles by railway, and the time occupied was twenty-nine hours. The landscape is not particularly interesting, being mostly flat and occupied for pastoral purposes, and there was a want of the picturesque appearance of cultivated fields and forests adjoining. I had to change carriages at the frontier of New South Wales, and pass my luggage through a formal examination by the revenue officials. The carriages of both railways are good. On my return to Sydney I found two more banks had closed their doors, and business practically at a standstill. The questions most anxiously discussed seemed to be how the deposits from home could be retained, while local deposits could be freed ; and how the banks could be changed into limited companies to save the shareholders from heavy losses. I could discover no feeling of sympathy for depositors at home who had their savings locked up in the banks, and who would suffer many hardships through being unable to get the use of their capital when they required it.

CHAPTER VIII

NEW SOUTH WALES

WE had arranged to visit the famous Blue Mountains near Sydney, and started for them on Saturday the 6th May. The first part of the journey as far as Paramatta is flat and uninteresting, but after two hours travelling we came to the first or little zigzag steep, and began the ascent of the mountains. The height of each station above the sea-level was painted on the name-boards, and at Springfield, forty-eight miles from Sydney, we found we had risen 1216 feet. At Lawson, ten miles farther, we had risen to 2399 feet; and at Wentworth, four miles more, we had climbed to 2856 feet above the sea-level; and at Katoomba, the highest point on the railway and sixty-two miles from Sydney, the line is 3349 feet above the sea. We stopped at Katoomba, and put up at the Carrington Hotel, a large and comfortable house, much frequented by people from Sydney and Melbourne in the hot season. The breezes on the mountain tops are cool even in the hottest weather, and the night air is very invigorating. The nights were frosty when we were there, but the days were delightfully warm and exhilarating. The scenery in the neighbourhood of Katoomba is unique in its way. The highest parts of the Blue Mountains are not ridges and peaks like those of most other mountains, but flat tablelands which present one strange peculiarity, that of portions of them having sunk many hundreds of feet, forming valleys as far as the eye can reach, the sides of which are walled in by sandstone cliffs of height so enormous as to be without parallel elsewhere in the world. The bottoms of these valleys are covered with dense vegetation, and from the cliffs above look like floors covered with rich carpets of harmonious colours, while through channels down the rocky sides of these valleys pour small cascades, leaping from point to point until lost to view among the lovely vegetation below, to form small rivulets under eververdant arches of graceful tree ferns and giant eucalypti. The Commissioners of Lands have formed footpaths to the bottoms of most of these valleys, and we descended 1700 feet to the bottom of one of them to see the marvellous beauty of the scenery, and were well rewarded for our trouble. Steps have been cut out of the sandstone, or where a little soil rests on some ledge, the steps are formed of branches of trees, and over all hangs a lovely roof of green leaves through which peeps of sunshine penetrate now and again; while on every fallen tree-trunk and mass of rock, mosses, green and gray of all shades, adorn and enliven the solitude of nature. We lingered in this valley of delight until the rays of the sun were becoming nearly horizontal above our heads, and then we found the ascent more difficult than the descent had been; and we had only time to escape from the shadows of the great rocks before the shades of night gathered around us. The valley of the Grose is the most wonderful of them all; it is a great chasm, the perpendicular walls of which are over 1500 feet high, and the depth to the bottom 2000 feet. It looks as if the centre of the earth had collapsed, and drawn with it a huge forest into perpetual repose beyond the disturbing foot of man. A waterfall, called Govet's Leap, falls in broken cascades down the almost perpendicular side of the valley, a distance of 2000 feet. The first fall of the water is 520 feet, and from that point to the bottom of the valley it rolls down like fleeces of carded wool. The points from which the best views of the valley can be had are carefully fenced round for the safety of visitors. Previous to 1813 this range of mountains was considered impassable, but in May of that year three explorers named Blaxland, Lawson, and Wentworth, penetrated a little beyond Katoomba after twenty days' hard work, and a tree, called the Explorer's Tree, is still carefully preserved by a wall and rail, on which they cut their initials, and under which they are said to have rested for a night. Next year they penetrated to the Bathurst Plains beyond the Blue Mountains; and shortly afterwards convicts were set to make the road over the mountains. Having spent four delightful days in this neighbourhood we returned to Sydney to prepare for our homeward journey.

Colonials of many years' experience say that society in Sydney is more continental in its habits and ideas than English. There are horse-races in Sydney every week-day throughout the year, and when the days are short, races are run by electric light. Betting is said to be the besetting sin of young colonials. Old-world affairs and history do not seem to interest the young people of any part of Australia, but cricket matches do. The laws of heredity are clearly observable in the characteristics of the descendants of some of the earlier settlers in Sydney, the "larrikin" of the present day being a direct continuation of a class deported to the Colony long ago.

On Sunday the 12th of May we went to service in the Cathedral. The most remarkable feature of the inside of that church is, that a space of about four feet all round the walls is being covered with memorial tablets made of glazed tiles, on which the virtues of deceased individuals are set forth in the best *post obit* style, at a charge of from twenty to fifty pounds per slab two feet square, according to the position which it occupies. That is surely an easier way of raising money than even by bazaars; and then if people have few virtues of their own, they can point with pride to those of their ancestors, enshrined within the sacred walls of the temple, some of whom, according to the tile slabs, possessed sufficient to have saved the city of Sodom.

In the afternoon we went to Bondi to see the Centennial Park and have tea with friends. This park cost £198,277, and was of course paid for out of a loan.

The history of a country always interests me as much as do its present inhabitants, as by knowing their past history I can understand something of their present characteristics. "Happy is the country that has no history," said a wise man; but that could not be said appropriately of New South Wales, because it has had a very interesting history for at least a hundred years. It is considered possible that Australia was known to the Chinese early in the sixteenth century, but the first authentic account of it is by Don Pedro de Quiros, a Spanish navigator who sailed from Lima in Peru in 1606 for the purpose of discovering a southern continent, in the existence of which he had a confident belief. It was visited by Dutch explorers in 1622, and by Dampier, an Englishman, in 1699; but it was in 1770 that Captain Cook, after his discovery of New Zealand, anchored in Botany Bay, and from that time its history begins.

The graphic account of his voyage published by Captain Cook, and his favourable reports regarding Australia and New Zealand, intensely interested the people of Britain, and as they had just lost their American Colonies, a new field for enterprise seemed opened to them. At the same time the home Government were feeling a difficulty in disposing of their criminal population; and early in 1787 Viscount Sydney, Secretary of State for the Colonies, determined to plant a colony in New South Wales. In May 1787 a fleet, consisting of six transports, small vessels of about 350 tons each, on board of which were packed no fewer than 564 men and 192 women sentenced to transportation, a small frigate of twenty guns, an armed tender, and three store-ships, was despatched to Botany Bay to found a colony, and arrived there early in January 1788. But Captain Philip, who commanded the expedition, found that harbour too exposed and shallow, and he moved his fleet into the bay now called Sydney Harbour, where the convicts were landed and the town of Sydney founded. From that time till transportation was abolished in 1840, 83,290 convicts were sent to Sydney. In 1831 the population was 51,000, mostly composed of people who had been transported there and their offspring; but in that year a system of assisted emigration was initiated, and the first two companies to arrive under that system were fifty young women from an orphan school in Cork, and fifty-nine mechanics from Scotland, whom the Rev. Dr. Lang introduced to aid him in building the Australian college.

Three years after transportation had been abolished a commercial crisis occurred, owing to the inflow of Government money having ceased. The Bank of Australia suspended payments, and its assets were disposed of by a lottery to save its shareholders from ruin. Now the Australian banks save their shareholders by converting themselves into limited liability companies.

The discovery of gold in 1851 was a most important event in the annals of the country.

Wages were low and work scarce at the time, and there was a general rush to the gold fields. Farms and stations were left without hands, and ordinary occupations were neglected. It was soon known over the world that great finds of gold were being made, and enterprising spirits from all quarters rushed to share in the anticipated prosperity. From that time the Colony has advanced by leaps and bounds.

In 1850, 976 vessels of a tonnage of 234,215 entered the ports of New South Wales, and 1014 vessels of 263,849 tons sailed from there. In 1891, 3021 vessels of 2,821,898 tons entered, and 3100 vessels of 2,872,338 tons left ports in the Colony.

Up till 1881 the trade of the Colony was practically in British hands, but since then I find the foreign tonnage has increased from 172,855 tons to 791,629 tons in 1891, but still the tonnage under the British flag is 86 per cent of the whole.

The value of the imports in 1850 was £2,078,338, and of the exports £2,399,580. In 1891 they had risen to £25,388,397 and £25,944,020 respectively. But gold sent from other Colonies to be minted was dealt with as imports and exports, and the enormous sums of money borrowed in London and elsewhere were dealt with as imports also.

Of the imports into New South Wales in 1891, £10,588,230 came direct from the United Kingdom, £11,127,178 came from the other Australian Colonies, £766,947 from other British possessions, and £2,909,042 from foreign countries. Of the exports from the Colony, £8,855,465 went direct to the United Kingdom, £11,603,170 to the other Australian Colonies, £607,970 to other British possessions, and £4,877,414 to foreign countries. The classification of the imports was as follows:—

Food and Beverages	£3,658,780
Wines and Liquors	991,163
Live Stock	1,336,771
Wool and other Animal Products	2,850,163
Clothing and Textile Fabrics	5,740,362
Minerals and Metals	2,283,858
Coals and Coke.	442,944
Specie and Precious Metals	2,503,222
Articles of Education and Art	1,259,975
Manufactured Articles not elsewhere included	3,979,359
Unclassified Articles	336,600

In 1891 the exports were nearly £4,000,000 over those of 1890, owing partly to the great strikes which in 1890 kept exports back. The exports were classed as follows:—

Animal and vegetable products, including wool	£12,126,357
Gold, Silver, and other Precious Metals	4,923,381
Live Stock	1,478,803
Coal and Coke	1,313,861
Other Minerals	605,501
Wines	21,077
Clothing, etc.	12,671
Other Unclassified Articles	125,367

The imports from the United States amounted to about £2,500,000, but the States took only

£583,723 in the produce of the Colony, and were paid the difference in gold coin and bars; and, as a contrast, Belgium took goods of the value of £1,039,723, chiefly wool, while the Colony took only £188,277 from that country, principally in the form of iron-wire bars and plates.

From Germany the imports were £773,016, and the exports to that country £437,522.

To France was sent £480,599, mostly wool, and from France £120,321 was bought. All the exports have fallen enormously since these tables were compiled, but the data are so far unavailable.

The amount of duty paid on imported spirits in 1891 was £869,513; on tobacco, £409,069; and on tea at 3d. per lb., £120,326. The total customs revenue for the year was £2,539,480.

The disposal of Crown lands previous to 1831 rested solely with the Governor, and large areas were granted to naval and military officers and men and free settlers; but in 1831 a system of selling the lands by auction was introduced, and in 1884 and 1889 new Acts for the disposal and occupation of land were passed on very much the same lines as those obtaining in New Zealand.

The value of the land sold between 1862 and 1891 was £45,837,717, the acreage being 35,270,331, and the average price 26s. per acre. The acreage under cultivation is 840,896, or only 2 per cent of the land disposed of.

New South Wales

Success in agricultural operations in New South Wales is altogether independent of the fitness of the soil for cultivation. So far experience has shown that an irregular rainfall and the want of uniformity in the seasons, which are the chief characteristics of the climate, are the greatest drawbacks to the advance of agriculture. Only 0.4 per cent of the total area of the Colony is devoted to the growth of agricultural produce; and, including that under artificial grasses for dairy farming, only 0.6 per cent, or 1.0 acre per head of the population, is under cultivation in any form. Taken as a whole, the yield of crops in New South Wales is equal to that of any of the other Colonies in Australia; but communication with the seaboard is more expensive and difficult, and stock rearing is therefore far more remunerative. The average production of wheat was, in 1888-90, 4.8 bushels per acre. The average from 1862 to 1892 was 13.1 bushels per acre. The yield varies from 18.2 along the north coast to 9.8 in the western district. The estimated value of agricultural produce for the years 1891-92 was £3,584,490, of which

Wheat represented	£759,708
Maize	667,532
Sugar	138,493
Oranges	86,812
Grapes and Wine	211,610

Comparing the whole Australasian Colonies, the average yield of wheat per acre for the last twenty years is as follows:—New Zealand, 25.59 bushels; Tasmania, 18.13; New South Wales, 13.74; Queensland, 12.20; Western Australia, 11.81; Victoria, 11.07; and South Australia, 7.46.

The number of sheep in New South Wales in 1891 was 61,831,416, and the value of wool exported £11,036,018, but that was largely in excess of any other year. In 1890 the value was £8,991,396.

A comparatively small export trade is done by New South Wales in frozen meat, cheese, and butter.

The population of the Colony in 1891 was 1,165,300, and of these 502,983 were adherents of the Church of England, 286,917 of the Church of Rome, 109,383 were Presbyterians, 110,110 Wesleyans, and 37,220 Congregationalists and Baptists. The remainder belonged to six other creeds. Education is almost free, and the estimate for that department, which is presided over by a Minister of State, in 1893 was £919,541. A fee of 3d. per week is charged each scholar, and in 1892 that yielded an income to the department of £75,913. Children attending school travel free by railway.

The number of arrests for crimes was 44,854. The divorces were 31.6 for every 100,000 married couples, and in Victoria 23.8, while in Great Britain the number was only 8.6; but in the United States of America there were 200 per 100,000. There were in the Colony 100 males for every 85 females, the excess of males being between twenty and fifty years of age. Excluding the aborigines, 725,015 of the population were born in the Colony, 266,101 in the United Kingdom, of whom 149,232 were in England, 4997 in Wales, 75,051 in Ireland, and 36,821 in Scotland. The Germans numbered 9563, the French 2030, and the Scandinavians 3397. The death-rate averaged for the last twenty years 16.35 per thousand per annum. In Queensland it was 17.04, in Victoria 15.56, in Western Australia 16.59, in South Australia 13.62; but in the city of Sydney it was 22.17. In 1891 the death-rate in England was 19.5, in Scotland 19.7, and in Ireland 18.2 per thousand. The illegitimate births were, in Sydney, 18.5 per cent, and in the country districts 3.80 per cent.

The duty on imported spirits, wines, and beer in 1892 amounted to £970,000, and on home-made beer, whisky, etc., to £158,000. No duty is paid on home-grown wines. The consumption of proof gallons of spirits was 2.83 gallons per head of the population, while in Victoria it was 3.93, and in New Zealand 1.74 gallons per head.

The bankruptcies in 1891 numbered 1238,

with liabilities amounting to £989,778, and nominal assets of £454,211. In 1892 the failures were 1243, with liabilities £1,203,685 and assets £540,726.

There are 2185 miles of railway in the Colony, which have cost £33,312,608, an average of £12,974 per mile, as against £43,955 per mile in the United Kingdom, where land has to be paid for at extravagant rates.

The net earnings are said to be 3.581 per cent on the cost, but as nearly all renewals of lines and plant have been paid for out of loans, and little allowance seems to be made for depreciation, it is difficult to say what the net earnings really are. For instance, £1,000,000 of the 1889 loan was spent in the "reconstruction and improvement of rolling stock and permanent way," and of the 1892 loan £200,000 was spent "on rolling stock, and towards fitting continuous brakes to goods carriages." (See page 63 of *Loans Expenditure*, issued to Parliament of 1893).

According to the *Statement of the Particulars of the Public Debt of the Colony on* 31*st December* 1892, issued to members of Parliament with the estimates, the amount of loans issued to that date was £62,573,703, which had realised the net sum of £60,395,869; and in his Budget speech on the 19th October 1893, Sir George Dibbs stated that the revenue for the year then ended was £980,000 less than that of the previous year, leaving a floating debt of £1,500,000.

In the *Estimates of Expenditure for* 1893 the sum of £1,862,630 is put down for "Interest on debentures and funded stock, £70,000 for railway loan of 1867, £82,116 for interest on treasury bills for deficiencies previous to 1886, and £141,875 for interest on treasury bills under Act 55 Victoria," a total of £2,156,621 for interest on public loans; and Mr. Coghlan, the Government Statist, estimates that, apart from the public borrowings, the sum due to "private creditors and absentees" amounts to £57,256,000, on which the interest is estimated to be £3,450,000. The interest payable to persons resident outside the Colony is estimated at £5,326,800. The public revenue for 1891 was £10,036,185, but for 1893 it was only £9,494,000. The expenditure in 1891 was £10,586,000, in 1893, £9,727,000. The estimates for 1894 are, income £9,971,000, and expenditure £9,854,000, and the sources of income are stated to be from railways, telegraphs, post office, etc., £4,590,000; taxation, £2,965,000; lands to be sold, £2,106,000; stamps, etc., £260,000.

The sales of land in 1891 were £1,163,338, and in 1892 £1,099,536, but I have not been able to procure the returns for 1893. As the sales of land become small, taxation must in-

K

crease enormously to meet the expenditure, and at the same time the security to lenders must decline proportionally. Deficiencies in the yearly budgets are being met by further borrowings. Large sums of borrowed money have been spent in renewing and repairing property which had been paid for by borrowed money before. The following items will show what I mean. Out of the 1860 loan, £5000 was spent "for repairing the Circular Quay at Sydney," and £1300 was spent on it again in 1861. In 1870, £5000 was spent for "repairing the breakwater at Newcastle," and £35,000 on "Relaying railway line, Sydney to Paramatta;" and dredgers for rivers and harbours are renewed from loans frequently.

In 1883 the Circular Quay was again requiring repaving, and £18,500 was paid for that purpose out of that year's loan, and an additional sum of £9000 was paid in 1886 for the same purpose. For wood-paving Elizabeth and George Streets in 1892, £22,000 was paid out of that year's loan; and from 1883 to 1893, £60,500 was paid out of loans for dredgers for Sydney Harbour alone. Out of the loan of 1890, over £250,000 was spent on "Making storm water channels" along several roads, an asset certainly not easily realisable, and in the same year £5000 was spent in building a "Morgue" in Sydney, and £6000 for draining Rockwood Necropolis; so that, while the

Sydney people live they are surrounded by the productions of borrowed money, and when they are dead they rest in ground drained by borrowed money.

The new Post Office in Sydney cost £562,021, and after it was built, the street in front of it was considered too narrow, and the whole opposite side, which was composed of valuable warehouses, was bought and pulled down to show off the handsome new building to advantage. I could not ascertain how much the transaction cost, but in the assets of the Colony there is a credit entry for £528,970 : 1 : 4 to be realised for the ground in New Post Office Street, or something, I believe, like £150 per square yard.

CHAPTER IX

VICTORIA

We left Sydney for Melbourne on 15th May in the P. and O. Company's steamer *Ballarat*, commanded by Captain Angus, an excellent type of a gentleman and seaman.

Tuesday, the 16th, we sailed along the uninteresting coast of Australia, and on Wednesday, the 17th, we again arrived in Melbourne, and put up at Menzies's Hotel while the *Ballarat* was taking in cargo. We spent the evening at Mr. Duncan Love's. Thursday, the 18th, I was occupied in business calls, and my wife and daughters spent the day with Lady Sargood. The last two banks to fail had closed their doors on the 15th, and the faces of business men had become so long that it was said the barbers were charging a penny extra for shaving them! Rumours of commercial disasters were very prevalent, and it had become ascertained facts that many well-known business men who were wealthy a year or two ago had lost all their fortunes, and others had suffered heavy losses through the failure of concerns in which they were shareholders.

Still life in the homes of most people went on as usual. In the evening we dined with Mr. and Mrs. Beath, at their residence in St. Kilda, and spent a very pleasant time with them and their family. Mr. Beath is another Scotsman who has had a very successful career in Melbourne, and who is held in high esteem for his business abilities and private worth.

Friday, the 19th, was a beautiful day, and we made several calls on friends early in the forenoon. My wife and daughters lunched with Mr. and Mrs. Robertson, while I went to the Australian Club with Mr. Paterson and Mr. Bruce, on whose nomination I had again been made an honorary member for another month. In the evening we dined with Mr. and Mrs. Barlow, and added another very delightful one to our many evenings spent in the company of friends in Melbourne.

Like all other large cities, Melbourne has its fashionable promenade, which is called "The Block," a part of Collins Street between Elizabeth and Queen Streets; and there from one to three o'clock daily the youth and beauty of Melbourne are to be seen, and for types of physical excellence they could take their place on equal terms with the same class in any city in Europe, while their manner and style possess a delightful freedom and freshness not to be met with in Pall Mall, the Bois-de-Boulogne, the Corso, or Princes Street.

On Saturday forenoon several friends called at our hotel to say farewell, and others met us at the railway station to see us off, while two or three accompanied us to the steamer, to all of whom we felt much indebted for their extreme kindness. We left Williamstown Wharf at 1 o'clock for Adelaide, the next stage of our homeward journey.

The first permanent settlement in Victoria was founded at Portland Bay by Mr. Edward Henty from Tasmania, who landed there on the 19th November 1834. Others followed, but the absence of good land in the vicinity of the port caused it to be considered an unsuitable site for a town, and the capital was eventually founded at the northern end of Port Philip Bay in May 1835, by two parties, one led by John Batman and the other by John Fawkner. These were soon followed by other parties from the same island and from Sydney. In October 1836 Captain Lonsdale was sent from Sydney to act as Resident Magistrate of the Port Philip district. In 1837 Sir Richard Bourke arrived from Sydney, and gave the name of Melbourne to the first town of the new settlement, and in 1842 it was incorporated as a town by an Act of the Legislature of New South Wales (13 Victoria, No. 40).

In 1857 Port Philip district was separated from New South Wales and erected into an independent Colony under the name of "Victoria." In July and August of the same year gold was discovered in Ballarat and other districts. A constitution giving responsible government to the Colony was proclaimed on the 23rd November 1855. The population was then 364,000. The area of the Colony of Victoria is 87,884 square miles, while that of New South Wales is 309,175, of Queensland 668,224, of Western Australia 975,920, of South Australia 903,425, of Tasmania 26,375, and of New Zealand 104,235. Added together, the area of the Australasian Colonies is only 680,764 square miles less than that of the Continent of Europe; and, excluding the territory of Alaska, they are larger than the United States of America by 47,647 square miles. The population of Victoria in April 1891 consisted of 598,414 males and 541,991 females. The Chinese numbered 9377, and the aborigines 565 as against 780 in 1881. Of the population, 713,585 were born in the Colony, 157,813 in England, 5094 in Wales, 50,667 in Scotland, and 85,307 in Ireland.

The Church of England had 401,604 adherents, and the Presbyterian Church of Victoria 163,149; the Methodist Church 150,000, and the Independents and Baptists numbered 49,993. There were 240,310 Roman Catholics, 6459 Jews, and 6746 Buddhists. Of the smaller denominations there was one "converted Jew," but to what he had been converted is not stated. Other fifty denominations had only one adherent each. The Gaelic Church had one representative, and the Puritan Church one. There was one Nazarene, one Morisonian, one Glassite, one Fakir, and one "Servant of God." One who believed in Moses and his laws, and one in the Church of the Future. Only one believed in Universal Brotherhood, and another in Conditional Immortality. One returned himself as Orthodox, and only two ladies and two gentlemen considered themselves Moralists. In the whole population there were only two Infidels and four Sceptics; but, stranger still, only three whose religion was "£. s. d."

Education in the Colony is compulsory, undenominational, and *free;* but the cost to the State in 1891-92 was £808,171.

The urban population at the end of 1892 was estimated to be 686,026, and the rural 471,652. Of the whole population 43.05 per cent resided in Melbourne. There were at the same time 23,526 men employed in gold mines. In Melbourne and suburbs the death-rate in 1892 was 20.65 per thousand. Of the deaths in the Colony in the same year phthisis caused 1483, pneumonia 1126, heart disease 1093, bronchitis 982, cancer 699, typhoid fever 356, and diphtheria 326. The mean temperature of Melbourne in 1891 was 57.6°, but it varied from 33.9° to 103.0° in the shade. The average rainfall is about 26 inches. In Sydney the rainfall is much higher, sometimes, as in 1891, being over 50 inches. The average rainfall in London is 24 inches, in Dublin 30 inches, in Liverpool 37, and in Glasgow 43 inches per annum.

The average production per acre of wheat, oats, and barley, in the Australian Colonies for the last twenty-five years is considerably under that of the United Kingdom ; in the Colonies it was —wheat 9.3, oats 25.6, and barley 18.6, against wheat 31.3, oats 38.8, and barley 34.1, in Britain. Victoria exported 6,853,195 bushels of wheat in 1891, while New South Wales imported 2,853,195 bushels. The sum of £682,501 of the money borrowed by the Colony of Victoria for irrigation purposes had been spent at the end of 1892, but none of the works were finished. The acreage which can draw supplies from these works when finished is 1,818,304.

The number of sheep in Victoria at the end of 1892 was 12,692,843, of horses 436,459, of cattle 1,782,978. In the United Kingdom at the same time there were 33,642,808 sheep, 2,067,549 horses, and 11,519,417 cattle.

The weight of the wool produced in Victoria

in 1891 was 76,503,635 lbs., and the value £3,957,901.

An idea may be formed of the enormous indebtedness of the Colony, by noting that for the eleven years ending with 1890 the imports averaged £19,455,019, and the exports only £14,491,137. In 1891 the imports were £21,711,608, and the exports £16,006,743. In that year New Zealand was the only Australasian Colony from which the exports exceeded the imports, and these were £7,331,496 against £6,986,348.

The value of gold raised in Victoria in 1891 was £2,305,600, but the value per miner was only £97:0:6, showing that the present production of gold does not pay the cost of raising it. For alluvial diggers the production was only £69:19:5; but for quartz miners, where machinery is largely employed, the value of the gold raised was £119:9:8 per man employed. The Colony gets the value of the labour in the mines, and the shareholders in mining companies at home pay the cost. The companies showing a profit in 1891 paid dividends amounting to £515,947, but no estimate of the capital invested in mining companies is available. The machinery in use, however, was valued at £1,848,218. The agricultural produce of the Colony in 1891 was valued at £7,770,658, and the animal production at £10,237,952.

Victoria

The revenue of Victoria for 1891 was £8,843,588, and the expenditure £9,128,699; but for the last two years the revenue has been very much less, and large sums have been borrowed to meet the deficiencies. The import duties on certain manufactured goods are so high as to prohibit their importation, and the Colony will require to reduce these duties very much to enable them to raise a revenue to meet their requirements.

The public debt of Victoria at the end of 1891 was £43,610,265, of which £2,603,800 had been borrowed at 5 per cent, £5,000,000 at 4½ per cent, £26,006,445 at 4 per cent, and £10,000,000 at 3½ per cent, and of the total interest of £1,745,449, £1,563,783 was payable in London, at an additional expense of 1.67 per cent on the interest. Of the £3,000,000 applied for in the London money market in 1891 only £2,000,000 were taken up. The public debt of the Colony now is nearly £50,000,000, of which £1,391,565 has been borrowed in the Colony. In 1891 the loss on the railways was £291,273, and on the post and telegraph department £109,009. The net revenue of the railways in 1891 was equal to 2.64 per cent, but the alterations on plant, renewals of lines, etc., was paid out of loans. Of the net proceeds of the loans up to the end of 1890, £34,460,233 had been spent on railways, £3,011,325 on water-supply for Melbourne, £4,181,636 on water-supply for country towns, £579,544 on Parliament Houses and Law Courts, £162,280 on public offices, £98,299 on defences, £1,177,495 on State school buildings, £121,445 on a bridge across the Yarra, £341,819 on the Alfred graving dock, and £259,091 on harbour works.

The private and municipal debts of the Colony must be twice as much as the public debt.

Residence in the Colony for one year entitles every male subject of full age to be registered as a voter. The Colony has two Legislative Chambers. For the membership of the Lower House, full age and two years' residence in the Colony is required; and for members of the Upper House, a free income of not less than £100 from freehold property. The latter are elected by persons paying not less than twenty-five pounds of rent per annum, or possessed of property worth not less than ten pounds of yearly rent.

The Lower House consists of ninety-five members, and the Upper House of forty-eight members, and there are ten responsible ministers. Members of the Upper House of the Legislature are not paid for their services, but members of the Lower House receive £300 each per annum.

CHAPTER X

SOUTH AUSTRALIA

WE arrived at Largo Bay at 11 A.M. on Monday the 22nd May, and went to Adelaide, the capital of South Australia, by the 12.30 P.M. train. Adelaide is finely situated on level ground surrounded by hills. Its streets are wide, well paved, and well kept. Round the city proper is a belt of unoccupied land about a mile wide, called the Domain, a public park in fact, and outside that space are the suburbs of the city, beautifully situated on ground rising towards the hills. Adelaide has fine botanical and zoological gardens, a technical college, and some other good public buildings, including the Houses of Parliament. The population of the Colony of South Australia in 1891 was 320,723, of whom 164,993 were males and 155,730 females, and of the city of Adelaide 133,252, equal to 41.59 of the entire population of the Colony. The Colony extends from the extreme south to the extreme north of the Australian Continent, and so far at some points has its eastern and western boundaries defined by degrees of longitude only. Like the other Australian Colonies, it has borrowed freely, and at the end of 1891 had a public debt of £21,133,300, of which £11,398,839 had been spent on railways. The revenue in that year was £2,829,453, and the expenditure £2,768,353. The value of the imports was £9,956,542, and of the exports £10,512,049. Of the Crown lands 12,802,180 acres have been disposed of. In the same year the acreage under tillage was 2,533,291, and the amount of wheat raised 6,436,488 bushels. The wine crop produced 801,835 gallons. One of the best authorities on Australian wines, Mr. Burgoyne, informed me that owing to the vines not being the best suited to the soil, and to the want of care in classing the grapes before pressing them, the value of the wine is very small compared to what it might and ought to be; and the same remarks apply to the 1,554,130 gallons produced in Victoria, 913,107 in New South Wales, 168,526 in Queensland, and 168,526 in Western Australia. The value of gold produced in South Australia in 1891 was £125,529, and the total previous production £1,174,296. There are 7,646,239 sheep, 188,587 horses, and 399,077 cattle in the Colony. The value of wool exported in 1891 was £2,166,125. The South Australian Government does not publish statistics as do those of most of the other Colonies.

The weather was fine the two days we were off Adelaide; the sky was cloudless, and the temperature 73° in the shade. I would prefer Adelaide as a place of residence to any of the other large Australian towns.

On the morning of 24th May, when we were preparing to leave for Albany, one of the first saloon passengers, a gentleman over 80 years of age, died suddenly, and his body was sent ashore before we left. He had been in Tasmania over sixty years, and was going home to see a sister in London.

We had rather a rough passage across "The Bight," the weather being showery and dull, with a strong breeze of wind and a temperature of only 54°.

We arrived at Albany, the second town in Western Australia, at 8.30 P.M. on Saturday the 27th, where a number of passengers landed on their way to the new diggings near there. We left again for Colombo at 10 P.M., feeling sorry our tour in Australia, where we had received much kind attention, was ended, but with pleasant remembrances of happy days and pleasant evenings spent in the society of friends we shall never forget.

The people and the country were both different

to those of New Zealand. The large towns in Australia give the people there more of a city style, but it is not of the old world style. There is an air of youthfulness about the towns, about the people, about their ideas, and even about their modes of expression. Little of the serious side of life seems to trouble them, and their philosophy has more of the "eat, drink, and be merry style" than ours has. They have borrowed and spent money with the recklessness and energy of youth, and have been more anxious to enjoy the fruits of industry than to be cultivators of the tree; and that spirit may readily be seen in the amount of money borrowed for places of recreation, such as public parks, botanical and zoological gardens, and picture galleries, etc., which are more prized as pleasure resorts than for their educational value. To pay for these luxuries out of their incomes, as we do at home, never occurs to the Australians—oh no, they will rather borrow the savings of people in the old country and lay it out for their own enjoyment.

CHAPTER XI

AUSTRALIAN BANKING AND FINANCE

THE way in which most of the Australian banks have set up receiving boxes, called "deposit agencies," all over Britain, and after having secured all the deposits they could possibly get possession of by offering high interest and the security of unlimited companies, their suspension of payments, and proceedings to limit the liability of their shareholders to their creditors are so well known as not to require special notice; but it shows how ready they are to borrow and how uncertain their payments may be.

Early in the banking crisis, a leading colonial financier pointed out in one of their papers that the system of banking at home could not be carried out in the Colonies, as bills and convertible securities could not be had there for the amount of money in their hands seeking investment, and that the Australian banks must, for their future welfare, secure as debentures at long or interminable dates a large proportion of the money hitherto received on deposits for from one to three years; and his compeers have not been slow to act on his opinions and advice. That even under their present arrangements they will all be able to continue their business is not considered probable by those best able to judge; and, that there are some wonderful revelations in connection with Australian banking in store there is little doubt. The affairs of none of the suspended banks have been investigated except in a perfunctory manner, although all have been reconstructed.

Such a process could not have been gone through in Britain. The depositors in Britain were little considered in the rearrangements; and the Parliament of Victoria had very shortly before the banking collapse passed an Act, of which the following is a copy, and which is worthy of careful consideration by those taking an interest in Australian affairs, as it regulated the proceedings in the reconstruction of all the banks having their head offices in Melbourne:—

"No. 1269

"AN ACT TO AMEND THE COMPANIES ACT 1890

"1st December, 1892.

"Be it enacted by the Queen's Most Excellent

Majesty by and with the advice and consent of the Legislative Council and the Legislative Assembly of Victoria in this present Parliament assembled and by the authority of the same as follows (that is to say) :—

" 1. (1) This Act may be cited as the Companies Act Amendment Act 1892, and this Act and the Companies Act 1890 may be cited together as the Companies Acts.

(2) This Act shall be construed as one with the Companies Act 1890.

" 2. The Act mentioned in the Schedule to this Act is hereby repealed.

" 3. Where any compromise or arrangement shall be proposed between a company which is, at the time of the passing of this Act or afterwards in the course of being wound up, either voluntarily or by or under the supervision of the Court under the Companies Acts and the creditors of such company or any class of such creditors, it shall be lawful for the Court in addition to any other of its powers on the application in a summary way of any creditor or the liquidator, to order that a meeting of such creditors or class of creditors shall be summoned in such manner as the Court shall direct, and if a majority in number representing three-fourths in value of such creditors or class of creditors present either in person or by proxy or attorney at such meeting shall agree to any arrangement or compromise such arrangement or compromise shall if sanctioned by an order of the Court be binding on all such creditors or class of creditors as the case may be and also on the liquidator and contributories of the said company.

"4. Where no order has been made or resolution passed for the winding up of a company and any compromise or arrangement shall be proposed between such company and the creditors of such company or any class of such creditors it shall be lawful for the Court in addition to any other of its powers, on the application in a summary way of the company or of any creditor of the company, to restrain further proceedings in any action suit petition or proceeding against the company upon such terms as the Court shall think fit, and also to order that a meeting of such creditors or class of creditors shall be summoned in such manner and at such time as the Court shall direct, and if a majority in number representing three-fourths in value of such creditors or class of creditors present, either in person or by proxy or attorney at such meeting shall agree to any arrangement or compromise, such arrangement or compromise shall, if sanctioned by an order of the Court, be binding upon the company and its shareholders, and upon all such creditors or class of creditors as the case may be.

"5. The Court, on the application of the company or of any creditor or person interested in the company, before sanctioning any arrangement or compromise under this Act may order such meetings to be summoned and inquiries to be made as it shall think fit, and may alter or vary such arrangement or compromise and impose such conditions in the carrying out thereof as it shall think just.

"6. Every person who is a shareholder at the date of the holding of such meeting shall in the event of the said person transferring his shares in the company during the term of any arrangement entered into at a meeting summoned as in the preceding sections mentioned be liable until the end of one year after the expiration of the term of such arrangement or until the end of three years from the date of such meeting whichever shall first happen to contribute to the assets of the company for the purpose of paying the creditors or class of creditors bound by the resolutions passed at the meeting an amount not exceeding the amount which he would have been liable to contribute if the company had commenced to be wound up on the day prior to the holding of such meeting in the event of the existing holder of the transferred shares being unable to satisfy the contributions required to be made for such purpose.

"7. The word 'company' in this part of this Act shall mean and include a building society under the Building Societies Act 1890.

"8. Every building society under the Building Societies Act 1890 shall for the purpose of being voluntarily wound up be deemed a company duly incorporated under Part I. of the Companies Act 1890.

"9. Any company limited by shares may so far modify the conditions contained in its memorandum of association if authorised so to do by special resolution as to reduce its capital by cancelling any shares which have not been taken or agreed to be taken by any person or which have been forfeited."

It may interest some of my friends to know particulars of the settlements made by the banks which suspended payments, and a few other items regarding these institutions.

At the end of May 1892 the paid-up capital of the whole of the Australian banks was £16,754,991, and their reserve funds were said to be £9,159,591, but that item has been written off by all the suspended banks. The deposits were at the same time stated to be £112,863,807, of which £43,342,373 was due to British depositors according to Mr. Hayter, and the assets were returned as follows, viz.—

Australian Banking and Finance

Coin and bullion	£19,652,206
Landed property	5,598,766
Notes and bills of other banks	548,920
Balances due by other banks	3,967,951

regarding the last of which Mr. Hayter remarks at page 508 of the *Statistics of Victoria*, and Mr. Coghlan at page 700 of the *Statistics of New South Wales*, that that sum included balances due by the branches of two Sydney banks to their own head offices after they had taken credit for the assets of the same branches. All other debts due to the banks were valued at £142,941,265.

The notes in circulation amounted to £5,510,891, and these are a first charge on the capital and assets of the banks. In New South Wales banks may issue notes to the extent of their paid-up capital and the coin in their possession. The average rate of the dividend paid by these banks in 1891 was £11 : 10 : 2 per cent on their paid-up capital.

In 1891 the average charges for discounting bills were for 3 months 7 per cent, 4 months 8 per cent, and 6 months' currency 9 per cent per annum, while in England the average rate was £3 : 9 : 6 per cent.

The average rate paid for deposits by the colonial banks was 5 per cent, while in London it was £1 : 6 : 8 per cent.

The banks which suspended payment have

been reconstructed on the following terms, viz.—
The Commercial Bank of Australia, with its head office in Melbourne, suspended payment on 4th April and resumed business on the 7th day of May 1893. The old bank had a capital of £3,000,000, in shares of £10 each; the new bank has a nominal capital of £6,000,000, also in shares of £10 each, on which £4 is credited as paid, and the remainder of the £10 is to be paid up in quarterly instalments of five shillings per share extending over six years. Depositors have received fully paid preference shares for one-third of their deposits, and deposit receipts maturing five years afterwards for the other two-thirds. The British deposits were £5,683,938.

The English, Scottish, and Australian Chartered Bank, 38 Lombard Street, London, suspended 12th April and resumed 9th August 1893. The old bank had a capital of £900,000, the new bank has an authorised capital of £1,575,000. The British deposits were £1,000,649, and the depositors have had to take 4 per cent debenture stock for one-fourth, 4 per cent terminable deposits for one-fourth, and 4½ per cent inscribed stock for the other half.

The London Chartered Bank, 2 Old Broad Street, suspended on 25th April and resumed business on 10th August 1893. The British deposits were £3,500,000, and the depositors have had the option of taking preference shares or deposit receipts bearing interest at 4½ per cent, payable in two yearly instalments beginning in July 1898. The nominal capital has been raised from one to four millions.

The Australian Joint Stock Bank, Sydney, suspended 21st April and resumed 19th June 1893. The British deposits were £3,868,881, and are to be repaid in ten equal instalments, beginning in June 1897, and half-yearly thereafter, with interest at 4½ per cent per annum.

The National Bank of Australasia, Melbourne, suspended 30th April and resumed payments 23rd June 1893. The British deposits were £1,804,865, and the depositors have received deposit receipts for two-thirds of their claims, bearing interest at 4½ per cent, payable in equal amounts, five, six, and seven years from June last, and fully paid preference shares for the balance of their claims.

The Bank of Victoria, Melbourne, suspended on 9th May and resumed payments on 12th June 1893. British deposits £1,100,000, are to be paid, one-fifth in preference shares, and four-fifths in deposit receipts, payable at different periods from two to twelve years hence, and bearing interest at 4½ per cent.

The Queensland National Bank, Brisbane, suspended 15th May and resumed 2nd August

1893. To British depositors were due £4,561,247, and they are to be paid by twelve deposit receipts, each for one-twelfth of the sum due, the first to be payable in June 1899, and yearly thereafter, bearing interest at 4½ per cent per annum.

The Bank of North Queensland, Townsville, stopped payments on the 15th of May and resumed at the end of July 1893. The deposits due in London were only £150,000, and depositors are to be paid by deposit receipts bearing interest at 4½ per cent per annum, the first for one-fourth payable in July 1897, and the remaining ones yearly thereafter.

The Commercial Bank of Sydney had only £242,924 of British deposits when it suspended payment on the 15th of May, and these are to be repaid by four deposit receipts bearing interest at 4½ per cent, the first payable in June 1898, and yearly thereafter.

When the City of Melbourne Bank stopped payment on the 15th of May 1893, it owed to British depositors £3,261,634. It resumed business on 16th June, and the depositors are to be paid four-fifths of their claims by deposit receipts at five, six, seven, and eight years, and bearing interest at 4½ per cent, and the remaining fifth in fully paid preference shares.

The Royal Bank of Queensland, which closed its doors on the same day, opened again on the

7th August, the creditors having agreed to accept payment in four deposit receipts bearing interest at $4\frac{1}{2}$ per cent, and payable five, six, seven, and eight years from 1st July 1893. The amount due to British depositors was only £300,000.

The money poured into the coffers of the banks had been largely in excess of the ordinary commercial requirements of the Colonies, and therefore stimulated building and other unremunerative enterprises, causing them to invest their funds in a way which must ultimately lead to serious complications.

The apparent prosperity of the Australian Colonies for the last ten years was only an indication of the reckless way in which money borrowed by the Governments, the banks, building societies, and other institutions was being spent; and little actual accumulation of capital has taken place, except that imported by immigrants, taking the Colonies as a whole. Their national, municipal, and individual indebtedness has now brought about a financial collapse, and what they have to show for the capital expended is largely assets of doubtful value. The Governments have been the greatest sinners as regards borrowings. Large sums have been spent in public parks, botanical and zoological gardens, city halls, government offices and post offices, all of which are largely in excess of the requirements of their respective communities, and the interest on the cost of which will be a serious item in their future budgets.

It is not by borrowing money and building therewith fine cities that a new colony can be made permanently prosperous, but by extracting wealth from the land in the forms of mineral, pastoral, and agricultural produce. The true prosperity of all colonies must arise from the land, as the labour employed in its cultivation and improvement affords the greatest and most valuable product to society, and not only pays its own wages, but the rent of the land on which it is employed, and interest on the capital which employs it.

The earlier settlers in colonies usually get possession of more land than they and their families can cultivate, and having got possession of it at a nominal value, they can afford to give as wages a larger proportion of its produce than can be given where land is dear. High wages are therefore paid to agricultural labourers, enabling them to save money and become landowners themselves, and in their turn to employ more labourers; and such prosperity encourages marriages, the children of which grow up well fed and trained agriculturists to carry on the prosperity of the land; and agricultural prosperity and mining industries always call into existence aggregations of manufacturing and artisan labourers to form towns, and to supply the agricultural and rural communities with their requirements at lower rates than these can be imported for, owing to the heavy carriages and long distances from which they have to come. At the same time, these town communities afford a ready market for the rude produce of the country in their neighbourhood, and by giving a higher price for it than could be got by exporting it, they thereby increase the wealth of the rural labourers. But when that class of population has grown in excess of the requirements of the rural population it becomes a parasite and impoverishes the population it lives upon, and can only be kept alive by the imposition of protective tariffs which prevent the agricultural colonists from getting the advantage of cheap labour and capital elsewhere, and causing a loss to them of the difference between the cost of what they could import the goods for and what they pay extra to protected labour.

The old theory that to buy things produced at home was a national benefit, and to introduce foreign commodities a national loss, has long since been given up, as it is quite clear that the importation of foreign goods in the common course of traffic never takes place except when it is, economically speaking, a national good, by causing the same amount of commodities to be obtained at a smaller cost of labour and capital to the country.

While the land is so cheap, labour will always be so dear that the colonist can import from the mother country the more refined manufactures cheaper than they can make them for themselves, and the mercantile class, who are always ready to dispose of the produce of the Colonies to the best advantage in all parts of the world, are the proper parties to administer to the opulence of the producers of the goods exported.

The question of the relative proportion of urban to rural population required for the prosperity of a new colony depends on so many circumstances and conditions that no rule can be laid down; but it is clear that the present proportion of town to country population cannot be maintained in the Australian Colonies even by the aid of extreme protection.

At present Melbourne alone contains 43.05 per cent of the whole population of Victoria, Sydney 34.22 of the population of New South Wales, Adelaide 41.59 of the population of South Australia, and Brisbane 23.79 per cent of the population of Queensland, besides other considerable towns in each of these Colonies. A large proportion of the inhabitants of the whole of them have for the last ten years lived on the moneys borrowed by their respective Governments for public works; and when their populations decrease, as they are bound to do now that all the great public works are completed, and borrowings of moneys for such purposes having ceased, a heavy load of taxation will have to be borne by the rural population which will check their progress in wealth. At present only about 40 per cent of the revenues of the Colonies is raised by taxation, the revenue from land sold being the largest item; but when the land is disposed of, taxes must increase enormously, as has already been noticed.

Colonial Federation has been looked on by some Australian public men as likely to be advantageous to the Colonies generally; but I found all the business men to whom I spoke of the matter opposed to that arrangement, except those of Victoria. Each Colony is jealous of the other getting any advantage; and Sydney people would not hear of Melbourne being made the capital of a Federation, neither would Melbourne tolerate Sydney as their superior.

The great stretch of territory covered by the Australian Colonies alone would make it very inconvenient to have a central authority; and to include New Zealand and Tasmania would make the scheme unworkable.

CHAPTER XII

HOMEWARD

THE weather was fine all the week after we left Albany for Colombo, and the daily routine undisturbed by anything of note. Our daily runs were from 320 to 330 miles, according as the wind and the tide favoured us.

The afternoon of Sunday the 4th June was squally, and about midnight we entered the line of the south-west monsoons, temperature 80°, and weather wet. We crossed the equator at 4.30 P.M. on Monday 6th June.

We arrived at Colombo at 4.30 P.M. on Wednesday the 7th, and spent the night ashore with Mr. and Mrs. Walker, of Icicle Hall, their beautiful residence a few miles outside the town, and situated between the cinnamon gardens and the sea-shore.

Thursday, the 8th, we spent visiting places of interest near the town of Colombo and making purchases. We lunched with friends in the Grand Oriental Hotel.

We went on board at 4.30 P.M., and at 6 P.M.

sailed for Aden, very pleased to be again homeward bound.

From the time we left Colombo till we reached the island of Socotra we had a gale of wind and a temperature ranging from 80° to 90° in the shade, with a moist atmosphere which made everything feel damp and disagreeable, while the high temperature had a very exhausting effect.

We reached Aden at 10 P.M. on Friday the 16th June, and left again at 9 A.M. on Saturday the 17th. The night was very hot, and we lay on deck under awnings. The temperature at noon on the 17th was 85°, but a gentle breeze of north wind tempered it, and made the weather delightful. At 4.30 P.M. we passed the island of Perim lying in the Strait of Bab-el-Mandeb. It lies five miles from the Arabian and nine miles from the African coast. The water is very deep on both sides of the island. We passed through the channel on the Arabian side. Perim rises 245 feet above the sea, and is bare and destitute of fresh water. It is a mile and a half long, and has a harbour capable of accommodating 40 men-of-war within 100 yards of the shore. It was taken possession of by the British in 1799, but was abandoned in 1801. It was again reoccupied in 1857 with the view of protecting our way to India after the opening of the Suez Canal.

Sunday and Monday were fine days, with a temperature of 80°, a dry atmosphere, and a northerly breeze.

Tuesday was a charming day, temperature 81° and no wind, and we were sailing close to the Arabian coast, which is low and sandy; and along the shore the sea was of a dark blue colour as if saturated with indigo, but what produced the effect I could not discover. We passed the rocks called the Brothers at 5.30 P.M.

About 8 A.M. on Wednesday we passed a valley at the far end of which we would have seen Mount Sinai had the weather been clear, but the morning was hazy.

We arrived at Port Suez at 1 P.M., and after fixing an extra rudder, entered the canal at 2 P.M. We saw the place where Arabi Pasha's men cut the fresh-water canal to stop the supply of water to the English troops who had landed at Suez for the last Egyptian war; but Admiral Hewit filled the dry dock with water from that canal, and secured a supply till the Egyptians were driven off and the canal repaired. We grounded in the Suez Canal at 9.30 P.M., and it took half an hour to get afloat again.

We arrived at Port Said at 6 A.M. on the 22nd. After taking on board some coals we left again at 8 A.M. for Brindisi. The temperature had now fallen to 72°, and the sea was as smooth as a mill-pond.

Friday the 23rd was another charming day, with a smooth sea, a fine gentle breeze, temperature 74°, and a cloudless sky, and we sailed along the historical island of Crete all day, and felt much interested in seeing the island which, according to the Greek historians and poets, was governed by its own kings as early as 1300 B.C. It was conquered by the Romans under Metellus, and on the division of the Empire it fell to the share of the Eastern monarchs. In 823 A.D. it was conquered by the Saracens. It was under the rule of the Venetians from 1204 to 1625 A.D., when the Turks besieged it, and after a war lasting twenty-four years, captured it, and it now belongs to Turkey. The island attained its greatest prosperity under the Romans.

We sighted the coast of Morea early in the morning of Saturday the 24th, and at 7.30 A.M. passed the bay where the battle of Navarino was fought in 1827. At 8.30 we passed the island of Strivali, which has a lighthouse and a large Greek convent. The day was one of the finest we had had on our voyage homewards, and we sailed among the classic isles of Greece all day. At 2 P.M. we passed near to the town of Zante, which was nearly destroyed by an earthquake six months before, and saw the houses being rebuilt. The population of the town is about 5000, and it is built along the top of a small bay, and up the slope of a hill on which is a strong fortification. The island of Zante is about 24 miles long by 12 broad.

Both the ordinary and a species of dwarf vine, on which currants grow, are largely cultivated on the beautiful sloping ground along its shores.

Continuing our voyage, we sailed between Cephalonia and Ithaca, the former of which is the largest of the seven Ionian Islands, being about 30 miles long by 9 broad, and the latter 15 miles long and 4 broad. The chief products of these islands are wines, currants, and olive oil, which are exported in large quantities.

Ithaca was celebrated among the ancients as the principality and home of Ulysses, and on the hill of Actos tradition points out the ruins of his castle. The channel between these islands is very like Loch Long. We next passed the island of Santa Maura, and saw the white cliff, 200 feet high, from which Sappho, the poetess, leaped on finding her love for Phaon unrequited.

The Ionian Islands were formed into a Republic in 1815 under the protection of Britain, and they continued under that form of government till 1864, when they were ceded to Greece, and now form part of that kingdom.

We arrived at Brindisi at 6.30 A.M. on Sunday the 27th. On entering the harbour an Italian steamer called *Milo* ran right across our bows, and we struck her near the foremast, smashing one of her boats and doing other damage.

Our captain was said to be at fault, as it is a rule of the harbour authorities that no steamer is to follow another inside the harbour entrance at a less distance than ten minutes slow steaming. Having landed our mails, and some passengers going home overland, we left at 11 A.M. for Malta. At 3 P.M. we passed Otranto, a fortified town on the strait connecting the Adriatic and Mediterranean. It has a curious old castle and a cathedral built partly in the sea. Next forenoon we passed the Gulf of Catina, and about 1 o'clock the town of Syracuse, once one of the most flourishing cities of antiquity, but now reduced to a small town of dirty streets. It is still strongly fortified, and has a fine cathedral, formerly a temple of Minerva, and some other good public buildings. At 3.30 P.M. we arrived at Valetta, and at 10.15 P.M. left for Gibraltar, after having spent some hours ashore. Here we received particulars of the loss of the warship *Victoria*. Some years ago many English mercantile houses had branches in Malta, but they have all withdrawn now, and the trade is entirely in the hands of the natives.

On Tuesday the 27th, at 9 A.M., we passed the island of Pantellaria, which used to be a noted resort of Barbary corsairs, and which is now occupied as a convict establishment by the Italian Government. At 1 P.M. we passed Cape Bon near the Bay of Tunis, and at 2 P.M. Zembra.

At 5.30 we were off Bizerta, a sea-port of Tunis, which has been acquired by the French, and is now being strongly fortified by them. It is the most northerly sea-port in Africa, lying in 37° 17′ N. Behind the town is a lagoon about 15 × 9 miles, and having a depth of 40 to 50 fathoms, and the French are deepening the channel between this lagoon and the bay, and making it one of the finest naval stations in the world. The ground behind the lagoon rises rapidly to a height of several thousand feet.

At 7.30 P.M. we passed the Fratelli Rocks. The coast along which we sailed all day was hilly and well cultivated.

Wednesday, the 28th, we were too far off the coast to see any towns or places of interest, but the weather was beautiful.

At 11.30 A.M. on Thursday, the 29th, we sighted the coast of Spain, and as we neared it, found it to be high and broken into valleys running from the shore to high ridges of hills inland.

The valleys were well cultivated, and, judging by the number of peasants' houses within sight, appeared to be fertile. At 1.45 P.M. we passed Cape Gata, near the Bay of Almeria. The afternoon became hazy, and we could only see the high mountains some distance inland.

We arrived at Gibraltar at 4.30 A.M. on Friday the 30th June, but did not go ashore. The widows of several officers of the *Victoria* embarked for London with us, and we left for Plymouth at 8 A.M. A Manchester manufacturer, who came on board at Malta, died at 2.30 P.M., and was buried in Trafalgar Bay at 8 P.M. The burial service was read by Captain Angus in a very impressive manner.

Saturday, 1st July, was fine, and we were within sight of the coast of Portugal most of the day. We passed Lisbon about 11 A.M. In the afternoon vessels of all sizes, from fishing boats to ocean liners, were within sight, and we began to feel we were again drawing near to the centre of the activity of the world, our own island home.

Sunday, the 2nd July, was our seventh Sunday at sea from the time we left Sydney, and we felt much pleased it was to be the last of our present voyage. The Bay of Biscay had been like a mill-pond when we passed through it. Off Cape Finisterre we had some showers, the first we had had since we sailed clear of the monsoons.

We crossed the Channel on Monday the 3rd, and passed the Eddystone lighthouse at 3.30 P.M., entering Plymouth harbour at 4.30 P.M., where I landed, and went to London by the night mail to attend to business, while my wife and daughters continued their journey by the *Ballarat*, and arrived off Greenwich at 6.30 P.M. next day.

We had very few first class passengers on the homeward voyage, the number never exceeding thirty, and only eight or ten besides ourselves did the whole voyage from Australia to England. No entertainments committee was formed, and no series of amusements was carried through as in the *Oceana*. But all the passengers were very agreeable, and time passed pleasantly enough. The officers were very nice men, and did their best to make all on board as happy as possible.

Wednesday, the 4th, we spent in London with some of our good colonial friends again ; and after driving through the principal streets to see the preparations and decorations for the marriage of the Duke of York and the Princess May next day, we left by the night train for home, where we arrived safely next morning, to the intense pleasure of the other members of our family, who had missed us much during our long absence. And so ended the most delightful tour we had ever had, or are likely to have again.

www.ingramcontent.com/pod-product-compliance
Lightning Source LLC
Chambersburg PA
CBHW020257170426
43202CB00008B/410